ORIGINAL
JAGUAR XJ

Other titles available in the *Original* series are:

Original AC Ace & Cobra
by Rinsey Mills
Original Aston Martin DB4/5/6
by Robert Edwards
Original Austin Seven
by Rinsey Mills
Original Austin-Healey (100 & 3000)
by Anders Ditlev Clausager
Original Citroën DS
by John Reynolds with Jan de Lange
Original Corvette 1953-1962
by Tom Falconer
Original Corvette 1963-1967
by Tom Falconer
Original Ferrari V8
by Keith Bluemel
Original Honda CB750
by John Wyatt
Original Jaguar E-Type
by Philip Porter
Original Jaguar Mark I/II
by Nigel Thorley
Original Jaguar XK
by Philip Porter
Original Land-Rover Series I
by James Taylor
Original Mercedes SL
by Laurence Meredith
Original MG T Series
by Anders Ditlev Clausager
Original MGA
by Anders Ditlev Clausager
Original MGB
by Anders Ditlev Clausager
Original Mini Cooper and Cooper S
by John Parnell
Original Morgan
by John Worrall and Liz Turner
Original Morris Minor
by Ray Newell
Original Porsche 356
by Laurence Meredith
Original Porsche 911
by Peter Morgan
Original Porsche 924/944/968
by Peter Morgan
Original Rolls-Royce & Bentley 1946-1965
by James Taylor
Original Sprite & Midget
by Terry Horler
Original Triumph TR2/3/3A
by Bill Piggott
Original Triumph TR4/4A/5/6
by Bill Piggott
Original Vincent
by J. P. Bickerstaff
Original VW Beetle
by Laurence Meredith
Original VW Bus
by Laurence Meredith

ORIGINAL
JAGUAR XJ

by Nigel Thorley

Photography by James Mann
Edited by Mark Hughes

MOTORBOOKS

First published in 1998, Bay View Books. This 2006 edition is published by Motorbooks, an imprint of MBI Publishing Company, Galtier Plaza, Suite 200, 380 Jackson Street, St. Paul, MN 55101-3885 USA

MBI Publishing Company titles are also available at discounts in bulk quantity for industrial or sales-promotional use. For details write to Special Sales Manager at MBI Publishing Company, Galtier Plaza, Suite 200, 380 Jackson Street, St. Paul, MN 55101-3885 USA

ISBN-13: 978-0-7603-2702-9
ISBN-10: 0-7603-2702-5

Editor: Warren Allport
Designer: Chris Fayers

Printed in China

About the Author

Nigel Thorley is a Jaguar historian, editor of *Jaguar Enthusiast* magazine, and a director of the Jaguar Enthusiasts Club, now the largest Jaguar-oriented club in the world. He has written many Jaguar books, including *Jaguar XJ: The Complete Companion*. He regularly gives talks and seminars on the history of the Jaguar marque and its vehicles.

James Mann's photography has been featured in many automotive books, as well as *Classic & Sports Car*, *Autocar*, and *Autosport* magazines.

On the cover: Series I Jaguar XJ6 2.8

On the frontispiece: Series II Jaguar XJ 5.3C

On the title page: Series III Jaguar V12 Sovereign

Table of contents: Series I long-wheelbase Jaguar XJ12

On the back cover: Series II Jaguar XJ6 4.2 with Series III Daimler Double-Six

Contents

Introduction	6
Past, Present & Future	8
Bodyshell	11
Body Trim	26
Boot & Tool Kit	38
Interior Trim	44
Facia & Instruments	62
Electrics	72
Engine	77

Carburettors & Fuel Injection	89
Cooling System	95
Exhaust System	97
Transmission	100
Suspension & Steering	104
Brakes	107
Wheels & Tyres	110
Optional Extras & Accessories	114
Data Section	120

Introduction

It has been a very interesting and informative, yet difficult, task to write this book, for two reasons. Firstly, Jaguar's XJ Series was manufactured for no less than 24 years, a significant production period for any car manufacturer, and in that time over 400,000 examples were built. Secondly, inevitably there were literally thousands of major and minor changes over the years because of the need to continually upgrade and develop the model in a very competitive marketplace.

Wherever possible all such information and detail has been included in this book. However, it must be borne in mind that although Jaguar was, and still is, a relatively high volume manufacturer, many new car purchasers would have specified bespoke requirements. Obviously many of these cannot be detailed in this publication, although some examples of the more obscure items are quoted where known.

Much of the information used has come direct from Jaguar's own records and therefore should be completely accurate. However, there have been a few cases where records have been in some dispute. To some extent this is inevitable in such a large organisation with so many cars produced over the period. Although the factory records state that changes were made at specific VIN (chassis) numbers, there will always be exceptions to the rule when using up old stock or when changes had to be made before finished cars were dispatched.

Whatever errors may or may not have occurred in the records, it is a tribute to Jaguar that such records were kept at all and were protected. Despite the trials and tribulations of the merging of the company, initially with BMC and then Leyland to form British Leyland, the records were retained in Coventry rather than being spread around the 'empire'. I feel very privileged to have had the opportunity to work with the factory records and therefore must thank key personnel at Jaguar and also the Jaguar Daimler Heritage Trust, now custodians of the companies' heritage. Without the Trust's help it would have been impossible to write this book; with its foresight the history of the company and its products has been secured for the foreseeable future.

Much information was also gleaned from the original Jaguar workshop and parts manuals plus the incredible number of Service Department Bulletins, issued to the franchised dealers when changes were made and/or problems arose. These provided a wealth of information and a very valuable insight into the models' development. It is also important to mention the many brochures Jaguar put out on the various models; again a significant number of varying types and quality was produced. I thank collector and dealer Andrew Swift from Sheffield for his help in supplying missing issues and clarifying dates when brochures were produced. They clearly show design and specification changes during the period.

There were many other reference sources used, some of which conflicted with others. Wherever practical, confirmation has been sought in an attempt to clarify the true information and to be as accurate as is humanly possible when dealing with historic data.

In many cases the best sources of information have been the cars themselves. Fortunately we are dealing with cars from the very end of the '60s working through to the early '90s. It was surprising and particularly fortunate that we were able to identify so many fine and original examples still in existence, untouched by restoration or modification. Many thanks must be given to the owners of these excellent examples, without whom my job would have been even more difficult. Their names and cars are identified in the panel and I hope the success of this book will be a tribute to them as custodians of important artefacts of motoring history that serve to benefit so many for the future.

On the subject of the cars featured in *Original Jaguar XJ*, special attention should be addressed again to the Jaguar Daimler Heritage Trust, which also provided some of the vehicles. The JDHT was in the fortunate position to acquire the very last examples of certain models straight from the assembly line; this has helped my task considerably. It also provided other examples of original low-mileage cars that had been donated to the Trust by their previous careful owners. I must also thank the trustees for their foresight and dedica-

This group of ignition and auxiliary lock keys typifies the attention to detail within this book. Keys shown are Series I ignition and FS single-sided auxiliary (bottom left pair), Series II ignition and FT double-sided auxiliary (top left pair) and Series III ignition and 'leaper' auxiliary (right-hand pair).

My own experiences with the XJ Series came in 1968 with the public launch, when I drooled over the *Motor* and *Autocar* magazine road tests and contemporary reports. Then I visited my local dealer, Byatts of Fenton, in Stoke-on-Trent to carry out my own review of this latest and most fabulous Jaguar saloon. After that my first 'personal' approach to the model came around 1971 when my elder brother (also a Jaguar fan) acquired a secondhand 2.8-litre Series I and as a passenger I marvelled at the quiet refinement.

Many cars illustrated in this book are exceptional specimens retained by the factory, in the care of the Jaguar Daimler Heritage Trust. Here a Daimler Sovereign 4.2-litre Series II long-wheelbase saloon emerges from storage. The colour is British Racing Green, and optional extras include the vinyl roof and chromed wheels.

tion to the marque – another example of how Jaguar's heritage is being protected for the future.

I enjoyed the help and guidance of many individuals in preparing and researching this book. I apologise in advance for not mentioning them all by name but give them all my sincere thanks for their contributions. I must, however, give very special thanks to one individual, Dave Marks from David Marks Garages in Nottingham, a fellow member of the Jaguar Enthusiasts Club and a man I proudly call a friend. Not only is he a Jaguar 'nut' but his knowledge and expertise relating to the mechanical aspects of the XJ model range is undoubtedly second to none. Having owned numerous examples, restored many and maintained hundreds within the course of his daily work, Dave offered a very practical approach to the research and was able to identify and confirm many unusual elements.

My first XJ was also a 2.8-litre model, a 1970 car purchased in exceptionally original condition and a car I thoroughly enjoyed owning for a couple of years. After progressing through various other Jaguar models I returned to an XJ, a Series II 4.2, then a Series III Daimler Sovereign, a Series III 4.2, yet another and then to what I considered the ultimate, a Series III V12 Sovereign of 1986 vintage. I sold this car to a friend, in hindsight mistakenly, when I contemplated the purchase of something completely different. Later, after buying a Series I V12 from my brother, I eventually realised the error of my ways and bought back the Sovereign. My determination to keep it this time led to a total refurbishment over a 12-month period. Yet again, surprisingly, I eventually sold the car again – and now regret it again! Now I own another example, a Daimler Double-Six Vanden Plas. Such is the magnetism of the XJ.

Owners of Featured Cars

Jaguar Daimler Heritage Trust (1969 Sable Brown Jaguar XJ6 4.2-litre Series I, 1975 Turquoise Jaguar XJ6 4.2-litre Series II, 1976 British Racing Green Daimler Sovereign 4.2-litre Series II, 1978 Squadron Blue Jaguar XJ12C, 1991 Silver Frost Jaguar Sovereign V12 Series III and 1992 Black Daimler Double-Six Series III); Howard Seymour (1968 Pastel Blue Jaguar XJ6 2.8-litre Series I); Dave Casey (1971 Willow Green Daimler Sovereign 4.2-litre Series I); Christian Nanan (Silver 1971 Jaguar XJ6 4.2-litre Series I); David Glanfield (1973 Lavender Jaguar XJ12 Series I); Nigel Thorley (1973 Morello Cherry Daimler Vanden Plas Series I); Paul Langham (1976 British Racing Green Jaguar XJ6 3.4-litre Series II); Bob Brown (1976 Coral Daimler Vanden Plas 4.2 Series II); Tony Blackford (1978 Biascan Blue Daimler Vanden Plas Double-Six Series II); Paul Gover (1980 Chestnut Jaguar XJ6 4.2-litre Series III); David Mills (1982 Regency Red Daimler Vanden Plas 4.2 Series III) and David Rutt (1982 Daimler 4.2 Series III).

If this book reflects the pleasure and enjoyment that I have experienced with Jaguars, it can only be good for other enthusiasts of the marque. I truly hope that readers will enjoy the book and that it will provide them with useful information.

Nigel Thorley

Past, Present & Future

Jaguar had enjoyed unparalleled success in the early '60s with a diverse range of saloon models, all powered by the legendary XK six-cylinder twin overhead camshaft engine. It was therefore perhaps surprising that at the 1968 Paris Motor Show Jaguar should effectively bring in a one-model policy – the XJ6 – when introducing its new saloon for the next generation of Jaguar customers. Not even Jaguar could have envisaged that the body style would have a life span of 24 years and that over 400,000 would be produced. Nor could anyone have foreseen that two generations of saloons later Jaguar styling would once again take its lead from the XJ Series.

The XJ Series, at the time of writing, remains Jaguar's most successful saloon car range ever with the longest production run in years and in total numbers sold.

At its introduction in 1968 the XJ heralded a whole new ethos for Jaguar in marketing strategy, styling and some mechanical aspects – although to a large extent relying on tried and tested Jaguar technology. While the car used the existing XK power unit, the top-of-the-range model with the 4.2-litre version (as previously fitted to the 420 model), a new configuration of 2.8 litres was introduced alongside for tax-sensitive markets. Similarly, while the independent rear suspension took its lead from the E-type and Mark X, originally from 1961, front suspension was relatively new.

Internally and externally the XJ6 offered new ideas yet retained the best traditional touches.

The start of the story. This Series I 4.2, the personal car of Sir William Lyons, was one of the earliest XJ6s produced. The nose features the original style of optional fog and spot lamp treatment.

The end of the story. This Daimler Double-Six was the very last Series III produced, in 1992. Clever styling revision meant that the XJ retained the wonderful 'Lyons Look' throughout production.

Jaguar took great pains to ensure the brand new car was instantly recognisable by its external styling, by the design of its dashboard, and by the quality finish of leather and walnut. Despite the all-new bodyshell, from any angle the XJ6 was still a Jaguar even if the original cars did not show any Jaguar badging and lost that prominent curvaceous radiator grille.

The XJ6's predecessor, the Mark X (later re-badged 420G), while impressive by any standards, had always been met with mixed reactions due to its sheer size and bulbous styling. In contrast the XJ6 was lighter, shorter and narrower, yet lost little in internal accommodation while gaining significantly in the ride and handling departments. The other saloons the XJ6 inevitably replaced, the 240/340 (formerly Mark 2s), S-type and 420, provided the sportier side of Jaguar saloon car motoring but with limited internal space. While the S-type and 420 provided the rear suspension and engine for the new model, the 240/340 were effectively designed back in the '50s and were decidedly long in the tooth. Therefore, although the new XJ6 was substantially bigger, it was as fast, handled better and was more economical than the smaller cars it replaced.

The success of the XJ6 was instantaneous and it was voted Car of the Year. The combination of the Jaguar image, a competitive price of just over £2000 and a degree of refinement unsurpassed by any other car ensured order books were overflowing, confirming the decision to discontinue all

other saloon models. This was not immediate and the Jaguar 240, Daimler 250-V8 and Daimler 420 Sovereign continued well into 1969 and the Jaguar 420G into 1970.

Initially a 'Standard' version was advertised with a 2.8-litre engine, offering a reduced state of trim at a strategically lower price. As orders were not forthcoming, only a few prototype versions appear to have been turned out. The 2.8-litre luxury model also received mixed reaction. Inevitably it was under-powered compared with the more torquey 4.2, and some who did buy the 2.8 soon found hidden problems as they complained of engine maladies leading to holed pistons – a situation that never arose during the company's testing due to the very harsh way in which the cars were driven!

It did not take Jaguar long to 'Daimlerise' the XJ6. After realising that it was not detrimental to 'badge engineer' a Daimler out of a Jaguar (the 420 begat the Sovereign), the XJ6 was suitably 'Sovereigned' from 1969, replacing the last remaining model from the old stable – the Daimler 420 Sovereign. This was followed by the introduction of a long-wheelbase bodyshell to rectify criticisms of lack of rear passenger accommodation.

By 1972 the range was expanded further with the launch of the XJ12, featuring the V12 Jaguar engine first seen in the E-type Series III in 1971. Jaguar had designed the XJ6 bodyshell right from the start to take the 12-cylinder power unit so no structural changes were necessary. Not only were there conventional V12-engined Jaguars and Daimlers, but an ultra top-of-the-range luxury saloon, the Daimler Double-Six Vanden Plas, then came along. Jaguar was able to take advantage of the coachwork facilities of Vanden Plas, at that time part of the British Leyland empire. The Vanden Plas provided the ultimate in luxury accommodation and bespoke workmanship, a match for anything else on the market and, perhaps surprisingly, for the first time in Jaguar's ownership of Daimler, outclassing the top-of-the-range Jaguar version.

After 98,500 XJ6s and XJ12s had been made the model underwent its first major redesign in 1973 and became the XJ Series II. A strengthened bodyshell and revised trim were necessary to meet stringent regulations demanded by Jaguar's largest overseas market, the USA, and at the same time there was a 3.4-litre replacement for the troublesome 2.8-litre engine. Jaguar also offered for the first time a two-door fixed-head Coupé range based on the short-wheelbase floorpan. This came with Jaguar or Daimler identity and a 4.2-litre or 5.3-litre engine.

Although the Series I XJs arrived on the scene during difficult years for Jaguar, with the BMC merger followed by the British Leyland take-over, it was the Series II that took the brunt of the changes. Despite numerous problems with build quality, questionable colour schemes and major production difficulties with the Coupé, more of these Series II models were turned out than the original cars and the Coupés in particular later became the most sought-after models.

Although by this time Jaguar was already working on a brand new replacement for the XJ, for various reasons it was a long way from production and so another major revamp of the existing model was needed. The aim was to keep the car competitive but as economically as possible. For the first time ever Jaguar went outside its own styling studio, to Pininfarina in Italy, to restyle the bodyshell. The revised model, launched in 1979 and called the Series III, gave the old XJ another new lease of life. Although the Series III retained basically the same engines and suspensions, the new styling was much more modern, with flush door handles, much larger glass area, a plush new interior and improved headroom – plus a £12,000 price. Despite all these changes, this was still unmistakably an XJ and sales soared again.

Although still part of British Leyland, with the cars continuing to suffer from the maladies of poor quality control, the XJ prospered. Jaguar was helped significantly by the appointment of a new boss, John Egan, who took the company, its employees and the cars under his wing, instilling new confidence and a revised regime of 'quality first'. All this paid off, culminating in the eventual privatisation of Jaguar and the reinstatement and growth of the legend.

The late '70s initially saw a lack of concern for and interest in the Daimler marque, which was soon turned around alongside the adoption of the Sovereign model name for an upmarket version of the Jaguar. This would ultimately turn out to be the most popular model produced on the XJ theme. Further enhancements came with improved specifications and even a 'fleet' 3.4-litre model with tweed upholstery and straight-grained veneer. Surprisingly, even though it was common knowledge that a brand new replacement was to be launched for 1986, the Series III continued to sell in significant numbers.

Even after the introduction of the new XJ6 (XJ40) late in 1986, Jaguar had no difficulty in selling off the last of the six-cylinder cars. Even then the old Series III would not give up, the V12-engined models continuing in production alongside the new cars for several more years. Ironically sales were still booming while Jaguar was still redesigning the XJ40 to take the 12-cylinder engine. The last Series III Jaguar V12 left the production line in November 1991 and all cars were sold in advance. The Daimler derivative soldiered on even further to the end of 1992 and again all the final cars were built to outstanding orders – all of which speaks volumes for the esteem in which the Series III models were held.

There were many valid reasons for not continuing production of the Series III XJs. The cars were designed back in the '60s without the benefit of modern build techniques, which inevitably meant they took longer to make. They had to be upgraded continually to meet ever-increasing changes in vehicle legislation. Although the XJ Series saloons were very refined, the sophistication demanded by customers meant the models just could not compete in the '90s.

In total nearly 403,000 XJ Series I, II and III versions were made over the 24 years of production. This was a very significant and profitable range of cars for Jaguar, a range that no-one would ever forget. Fortunately the styling of the XJ Series would not be forsaken as, despite a contemporary move to the angular looks of the XJ40, Jaguar would refer back to and finally instigate a restyle in the X300 around the 'retro-curvaceous' looks of the Series III.

Future Jaguar saloons are also destined to get the 'XJ look' as Jaguar continues to review its latest design studies against the backdrop of successful previous models. The XJ is not dead but lives and will continue to do so, not only in the new cars the company produces but in the ever increasing band of enthusiasts for the models – ensuring the remaining cars are secured for the marque's future heritage.

Bodyshell

Like many of Jaguar's previous bodyshells, the XJ6 was produced by the old Pressed Steel Fisher company. It was ironic that the plant that produced this particular bodyshell, Castle Bromwich in Birmingham, would become part of Jaguar later in its life. The bodyshell was made up of small pressings spot-welded together to make the complete unit, in a similar way to the Mark X, which

it replaced. The Mark X shell had always been regarded as the strongest Jaguar had produced up to that time but the XJ6 would be even stronger.

The Mark X design had often been criticised for the exceptionally deep section of its sills, making it difficult to get in and out of the car. Although the XJ6 also featured similarly strong sill areas, their size was more acceptable. The

The original Series I XJ6 in its purest form. From this angle the only way to recognise this as the 2.8-litre de luxe model is by its lack of chromed wheel rimbellishers. Colour: Pastel Blue.

Another early Series XJ6, this time in 4.2-litre form. Although this Sable Brown car, chassis number 1L.1370, was built in 1968, at some point it has received the style of reversing lights and separate reflectors introduced in March 1970. As this was Sir William Lyons' personal car, perhaps he wanted it updated visually? A North American export version of the Series I XJ6 4.2-litre saloon (left), in Light Silver, with side indicator repeater lamps. Some cars for the US would also have been fitted with thick black rubber Nordel over-riders.

The long-wheelbase bodyshell of the Series I model is seen on this Jaguar XJ12, painted Lavender. The new V12 model had a much sportier grille (vertical slats only) with a prominent V12 badge. The Daimler Vanden Plas Double-Six Series I saloon (right) was the most expensive of all the Series I cars, and the rarest. All Daimler Series I models had this fluted radiator grille, but the chromed swage line trims, vinyl roof, remote-controlled driver's door mirror and fog/spot lights were standard features only for the VDP at this time. The colour is Morello Cherry.

The Series II XJ bodyshell, here seen in 4.2-litre Jaguar form. Revised frontal aspect – to accommodate higher bumpers – included a shallower grille. The colour is Turquoise.

The ultimate Series II model is the Daimler Vanden Plas Double-Six. Even at this time chromed wheels were still an extra-cost option. Unlike Jaguar models, Series I/II Daimlers always had a chromed strip down the bonnet. The colour is Biascan Blue.

whole bodyshell was lower than any previous Jaguar saloon, but good design still allowed the floor to be dropped as low as possible to provide reasonable headroom.

The strong front bulkhead used the heating and ventilation system ducting to provide extra bracing. This ducting used 'partitions' to help reduce noise transmitted to the interior of the car from the engine bay. Two very strong steel box sections, braced by the inner wings, ran from the passenger compartment to the front of the car. The front subframe was mounted on this structure. Further bracing was provided by a very deep and strong front cross-member which also supported the radiator.

The one-piece front wings were not welded but merely bolted on to the main structure, making for easier and cheaper repairs. Also bolted in position was the one-piece front under-valance, which held the chrome-finished under-grille. Two tubular steel diagonal bracing struts were bolted to the centre of the bulkhead and at midpoints along the inner wings to provide extra structural strength in the under-bonnet area. These struts were always finished in black and had to be removed for major engine work.

The one-piece forward-hinged steel bonnet was mounted via two hinges and was self supporting due to the counterbalance of its weight. The bulge in the centre of the bonnet panel, plus some cross-bracing, also helped to create extra strength. It was originally intended that the car would not feature this bulge – until it became clear that the 4.2-litre XK engine could not be accommodated without it due to its height!

The floorpan itself was significantly ribbed to add strength and the mid-way cross-member, on to which the front seats were mounted, was also substantial. Similarly another cross-member ran below the rear seat and in addition strength was gained from the roof section and door pillars, which ensured a very strong structure overall.

At the rear of the passenger compartment two further box sections ran up and over the rear seat pan, eventually meeting up with the double-skinned boot floor, within which was a separate ribbed section forming the spare wheel well. The box sections provided the mounting points for the rear suspension subframe assembly. Rear inner wings were welded in place as at the front and the rear outer wings were of one piece, again welded to the main structure.

The 4.2-litre version of the Vanden Plas Series II saloon, the only external difference from the Daimler Double Six model being the boot badging. This colour is Coral.

The XJ12 Coupé (facing page), here seen in Squadron Blue, was based on the short-wheelbase saloon bodyshell and floorpan. Vinyl roof was standard on all Coupé models, but the Kent Alloy wheels were an extra-cost option in this case.

However, the lower rear wing sections were entirely separate and bolted into position, effectively enclosing the area around the two side-mounted fuel tanks. These lower panels had to be removable to gain access to the fuel tanks. A rear valance was welded on to the main bodyshell, which was designed with holes to accommodate the rear exhaust pipes exiting from either side.

The ventilation system on the XJ6 was interesting in that Jaguar designers had come up with a unique method of extracting air from the interior, via a slot in the rear parcel shelf and out through a series of elongated slots in the double-skinned boot surround below the rear window.

Doors were of conventional construction using skins welded against the inner casing, and in keeping with Jaguar's usual practice the window frames were of separate construction and bolted into position.

The whole bodyshell structure of the Series I XJ6 came out with a gross weight of just 840lb, significantly lighter than any large Jaguar saloon before it.

The main structure of the bodyshell remained unchanged throughout Series I production but various minor changes took place. For example, in August 1969 seat belt anchorage points were

amended so that the cars could be fitted with inertia reel belts. In November of the same year, complaints of excessive heat being felt through the floorpan resulted in heat shields being fitted between the exhaust and bodyshell under the front passenger floor area. By October 1970 slight changes were made to the flanges on the front wheelarches after complaints that tyres had been fouling the wing edges.

No changes to the bodyshell were necessary when the Daimler Sovereign was introduced, and because the shell had been designed from the start to utilise the V12 power unit no physical changes were required either when the 12-cylinder models were introduced from 1972.

Jaguar countered complaints about lack of rear legroom by introducing a long-wheelbase version of the car from the 1972 Earls Court Motor Show. Offering an extra 4in of legroom in the rear compartment unfortunately increased the weight of the car. This did mean a slight drop in performance but nevertheless, despite the extra length, weight and cost, the long-wheelbase shells would eventually become the norm; the short-wheelbase version was dropped from the range early in Series II production, save for the two-door Coupé versions. The long-wheelbase bodyshell was an

Relatively early example of the Series III saloon (above), in this case a 4.2-litre Jaguar model in Chestnut. Mid-term Series III Daimler in Black (left), dating from the time when the company realised the importance of separating the Jaguar and Daimler marques. Using special hub caps and swage line chrome trims (from the VDP models) gave all the Daimlers some distinction.

Series III Jaguar Sovereign models in 4.2-litre (1986 Bordeaux Red car) and 5.3-litre (1991 Silver Frost Metallic car) guises. Despite six years separating them, revised boot badging was the only external change – both cars have 'pepperpot' alloy wheels. The sunroof was an extra cost option on Jaguar models right to the end of production.

entirely different structure – not the usual 'cut-and-stretch' – but the design concept was exactly the same, requiring only the addition of 4in longer rear doors.

In September 1973 major changes to the bodyshell were to take place with the introduction of the Series II XJs. These alterations were brought about by changing legislation and a need to rectify many minor flaws in the original design to meet ever-increasing demands from customers.

Firstly, due to changes in bumper height regulations in the US, the mounting and style of the front bumper had to be changed. This necessitated design changes to the front wings, bonnet and under-valance. The wings, although basically of the same style, were subtly different in shaping

and size with new mounting holes for the bumper. The side/indicator lighting units were now mounted under the bumper rather than above, and a new under-valance accommodated a larger space for a revised under-grille, which also allowed more air through to the radiator and engine compartment because the main radiator grille was so much shallower.

In other external areas the bodywork was pure Series I, with the same sills, rear wings, boot panel and rear under-valance. The doors, although still using the same outer skins, were redesigned internally to incorporate W-section strengthening steel bars to guard against side impact. These were deleted on all models built after March 1978, except those destined for the US and Japan.

Series I and II compared. The original purity of line was carried over to the Series II saloon, the later model's raised front bumper height the only difference from this angle.

Coupé clearly shows its pillarless construction with all windows down, and the addition of a vinyl roof for these cars. Compared with earlier saloons, Series III, always based on the long-wheelbase floorpan, has a taller roof line, larger window area, rubber-faced bumpers and recessed door handles.

The main structure of the bodyshell remained intact and unchanged except for the front bulkhead, which was completely redesigned to accommodate new electrics, heating and air conditioning systems. Instead of the previous double-skinned bulkhead with integrated ducting and holes through which all the necessary piping and connections were made, Jaguar engineers had worked miracles by opting for an entirely different approach.

Firstly, the bulkhead was now a single skin. To stop excessive heat transfer, pre-formed asbestos panelling was fitted to the engine side and pre-formed Oldfield bitumen panelling on the cockpit side. Secondly, holes were not now needed in the bulkhead to accommodate wiring and piping;

instead multi-pin sockets, into which the wiring loom plugged, were provided on each side. Rigid steel air ducting, built into the bulkhead, was connected at each end by flexible tubing; this also made servicing easier and gave further structural strength to the whole.

The Series II bodyshells were actually some 80lb heavier than the Series I.

As well as the conventional short- and long-wheelbase four-door saloons, the new two-door Coupé variant dictated an adapted short-wheelbase bodyshell of its own. The 'ordinary' bodyshell had to include an additional box-section strengthener behind the front door-shut face to put back the strength lost from removal of the B/C post to make the Coupé a true pillarless saloon.

Series I/II/III styling evolution seen from front. Tall Series I XJ6 'egg-crate' grille was not to everyone's liking, although the car essentially retained that Jaguar look of earlier '60s models. Series II, here a Jaguar 4.2, had raised front bumper, new 'under-grille' and shallower radiator grille. Series III, this time as a Daimler model with the more prominent fluted radiator grille. Particular changes are rubber-faced bumpers, integrated indicator lighting, revised under-bumper grille and valance, and adoption of headlamp wash/wipe.

The roof still provided part of the shell's strength and to ensure rigidity the rear quarter pillar was not only strengthened but also enlarged (hidden to some extent on the production cars by the fitment of a black vinyl roof covering).

New doors, now 4in longer than the saloon versions with accompanying strengtheners on the inside, had to be made up for the Coupés. In fact the doors were made up from a saloon door with an extra section of another door welded into place! Exactly the same door hinges were used on Coupé bodies, which is perhaps one reason why the doors often sagged. Internally the only changes to the shell were the movement of the seat belt anchorage points.

By the end of 1974 the short-wheelbase saloon bodyshell had been discontinued from all ranges, leaving the long-wheelbase four-door saloon shell and the two-door pillarless Coupé shell. The last short-wheelbase shells used on the Coupé were completed in November 1977, after which only the long-wheelbase shell for four-door saloons remained available.

March 1979 saw the introduction of the Series III bodyshell, an entirely new structure rather than a re-vamp of the old shell. Jaguar had used Pininfarina in Italy to restyle the XJ and extend its life until a new model was ready. Their brief had been to enhance and modernise the design but retain the essential 'Jaguar look'. This redesign cost Jaguar over £7 million.

The Series III bodyshell was therefore completely different from the Series II design. Starting from the top, this meant increased height allowing more glass area, inclining the front screen pillars by 3in to achieve this and lifting the rear section of the roof to provide a larger rear screen. Both front and rear screens would be bonded to the shell, improving structural strength as a whole. The availability of an all-metal sliding sunroof as an extra-cost option meant there were effectively two distinct bodyshells – with or without sunroof – for the Series III saloons.

The doors were entirely new pressings incorporating provision for flush door handles and, of

course, new window frames were needed. At the front the bonnet pressing was similar to the Series II's, but the under-valance was restyled and the grille revised. The front wings were subtly different below the headlamps although general shape was unchanged. Similarly at the rear, the boot pressing, fuel tank covers and under-valance were the same as Series II although the wings came in for some slight reshaping.

Apart from extra pre-formed sound-deadening panels in the doors and on the bulkhead and transmission tunnel, everything else on the body was very much Series II. That is surprising when one views the vehicles side by side today. Minor changes were made for the fixing holes of various parts both under the bonnet and in interior trim areas. Also with the fitment of various electronic items in the boot bulkhead area, this too varied slightly on the very last models.

The spare wheel well was also changed, eliminating the two inspection panels in the previous shell. The well was also made slightly deeper to accommodate the wider profile tyres and wheels used on certain models.

Bodywork detailing

All underside areas of the bodywork were painted body colour, although Jaguar did use a body 'schultz' spray, mostly in black, to give some protection against the elements. It is fair to say that most dealerships applied conventional underbody sealing, finished in black, prior to delivery to new owners. Since the introduction of the XJ Series, the use of specialised body protection treatments, such as Ziebart, at extra cost to owners was also encouraged by many dealers.

Boot and bonnet areas were always finished internally in body colour except for the early Vanden Plas models, which had final colour coats applied at Kingsbury in London. Series I and early Series II models of this type were built at Jaguar as conventional cars but then shipped down to Vanden Plas where the cars were repainted in their own bespoke range of colour schemes (see *Data Section*, page 120). This meant that areas like the engine bay were necessarily sprayed in black before assembly at Jaguar so as to avoid removal of mechanical and electrical items when the cars were resprayed in London.

Underbonnet sound-deadening varied during

Series I/II/III styling evolution seen from rear. Series I, showing revised reflector and reversing light lenses of later cars. Series II, seen on an XJ5.3C, was substantially unaltered, but boot plinth differs. Series III has new lighting, boot plinth, bumpers and exhaust pipes.

production. Series I models had black-finished ½in-thick coated felt. This was shaped to avoid any contact with the top of the engine or radiator and held in position by L-shaped steel supports in the bonnet. These supports were crudely shaped to avoid touching the engine cross-brace bars. On Series II cars the supports were redesigned with preshaped metal pressings for a better finish. Underbonnet sound-deadening was removed

from all S- and T-registered Series II models, leaving the finish in body colour and uninsulated. Sound- deadening returned later in other forms, and fasteners also changed.

Under-bonnet hinges, springs, locks, etc, were always painted body colour. However, the bonnet security release lever was always galvanised and unpainted. In the front inner wing areas on both sides strategic holes (normally covered with black

The very last Series III car produced by the factory in 1992 was this Black Daimler Double-Six with Kent alloy wheels.

Series I under-bonnet insulation panels (left) were thick and pre-formed to avoid contact with the radiator top rail or cam covers. Series II bonnet (above) was a different pressing, with elongated holes in the welded cross-support; thinner under-bonnet insulation was also used, eliminating the section at the far front of the bonnet area around the radiator area.

Two types of bonnet support strut, early (right) and late (far right), the change occurring during Series II production.

Gap differential between driver's door and front wing shows that panel fit from the factory was never perfect. This is a low-mileage Series III still in its original paint.

rubber grommets) were provided to allow access with a screwdriver to release the bonnet locks if ever the cable-operated release from inside the car should fail.

Bonnet stays, on either side at the front of the bonnet mounted to the inner wing areas, were initially a simple strut, with a detent necessitating release by hand introduced for Series II models. Later Series IIs and all Series IIIs were fitted with a much more sophisticated mechanism.

The two engine bay cross-brace bars fitted to all cars throughout production were always finished in black, with plain untreated metal nuts, bolts and washers to secure them. The body number was either stamped on the offside strengthener to the cross-brace (right-hand drive cars) or on the bulkhead cross-brace strengthener.

All XJ Series saloons should be fitted with black plastic U-formed finisher strips over the inner/outer wing joint line on either side of the under-bonnet area. Similarly, anodised colour trim was fixed over the joint forming the A-post water gutters (visible with the front doors open).

Many Series II models during the last two years of production had no under-bonnet insulation at all (above); instead the underside was coated in body 'schultz' and painted to match exterior finish. Series III bonnet (right) was also a different pressing, with elongated holes down each side strengthener and in the front strengthener. Bonnet insulation was now of a thin pressed foam style secured with visible clips.

Body Trim

Save for badges and minor decoration differences between Jaguar and Daimler derivatives, body trim remained fairly stable on each Series. However, over the years interchange between specifications made matters confusing. It is therefore best to deal with each Series in turn.

Series I

From the front, the look of the Series I XJ6 did not change at all throughout its production life. The single-piece, slim-line, chrome-plated bumper, with matching stubby overriders, was the same for the majority of markets (home and abroad) except in certain US states, where a Nordel pre-shaped rubber overrider had to be used. The chrome-plated mock horn grilles remained the same, as did the headlamps (except for right-hand and left-hand dipping, and again the need to suit US markets with a standardised 5in outer headlamp unit). The 'egg-crate' radiator grille with the centre plastic 'growler' (Jaguar's head) badge against an orange background also remained unchanged throughout Series I production.

The chromed outer headlamp surrounds differed on the earliest cars in that they were solid, being the type used on the previous 420G model. However, in 1970 fresh air inlets with on/off controls were fitted to the front footwell areas, the air supply coming through new mesh grilles in the outer headlamp surrounds. For the American market, 5in diameter headlamps with broader chromed surrounds were fitted, a feature that would continue for later Series as well. Headlamps were of the sealed beam type on all models except for certain export markets and the Vanden Plas models, where quartz halogen units were used as standard right from the start. These were later offered as an extra-cost option on late Series I cars just prior to the model's demise.

Sidelamp units were also different for some export models, with pure white lenses instead of the white/amber mixture required in the UK. The majority of export models also had amber repeater lenses with chrome surrounds on front and rear wings. These repeaters were never fitted to home market models.

Chrome-plated outer headlamp cowl surrounds changed during Series I production, the later type with mesh air intakes remaining in use to the end of the Series III.

The under-valance chromed grille remained the same for all models but the upper grille for the Daimler models incorporated a prominent chromed surround, fluted at the top in traditional Daimler fashion with an inset central plastic badge with a scripted 'D' in gold on a black background. The chromed slats were entirely vertical with no horizontal sections as on the Jaguar.

The bonnets of the more up-market Daimlers featured the extra adornment of a full-length central chrome strip, of triangular section, neatly meeting the top of the radiator grille to form a continuous line. Lastly, on the Series I Vanden Plas Daimlers the horn grilles were replaced by back-mounted rectangular Lucas fog and spot lamps, standard only on this model but available as an extra-cost option on all others.

Changes for the V12 models affected only the Jaguars; the Daimlers featured exactly the same frontal aspects for six- and 12-cylinder cars except for the discreet V12 badge encased in the top of the radiator grille surround. The Jaguar V12 radiator grille also used only vertical slats (like the

Series I/II/III nose badge evolution, from top left. 1) Original gold 'growler' badge used on all Series I XJ6 models. 2) Daimler motif found on six-cylinder Series I, II and early III models; note the shape where it meets the centre bonnet chrome strip. 3) V12 badge used only on Series I Jaguar V12 model. 4) V12 insignia used on Series I, II and early III Daimler models. 5) Revised 'growler' style for Series II/III Jaguar models. 6) Removal of centre bonnet chrome on Daimler models during Series III production brought different fluted radiator grille top and a new badge with scripted 'D' for all Daimler models.

Series I/II/III front wing badge evolution, from top. 1) Plastic rectangular 'leaper' badge used on all Series I, II and early III Jaguar models; these badges are handed due to the slight forward slope of the rectangle. 2) Later Series III 'leaper' badge for Jaguar models. 3) Only during Series III production did Daimler models receive a scripted 'D' badge. All of these badges should be mounted on a rubber gasket.

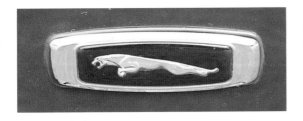

Daimler) but without the prominent surround, instead taking its more subtle surround from the XJ6 grille. Instead of the 'growler' badge a prominent centre rib contained a vertically-mounted, rectangular plastic badge containing a small gold 'growler' below which was an elongated 'V' followed by the word 'Twelve', also in gold, all on a black background.

Number plates at the front of the XJ Series I models were mounted on a black-painted metal surround, which was bolted directly underneath the bumper bar with U-shaped brackets. The mounting had a curved edge facing inwards towards the car.

A Jaguar 'leaper' (a stylised leaping jaguar), in the form of a slightly forward-sloping, handed, rectangular plastic badge, was fitted to the bottom rear of the front wings. The 'leaper' always faced towards the front of the car and was finished in silver with a silver surround against a black background. This type of badge was attached to the car via two plastic studs and a rubber gasket. Series I Daimler wings carried no badging at all.

   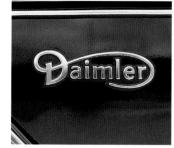

Series I/II left-hand boot lid badge evolution, from top left. 1) Early Series I models had no Jaguar script on the boot lid, but then this style (as used on previous '60s Jaguars) was adopted. 2) During Daimler Series I/II production the word 'Sovereign' was used, Daimler not featuring on the boot lid. 3) Introduction of Daimler Vanden Plas Series I brought this boot lid script, carried over to Series II models as well. 4) Introduction of fuel injection brought an additional badge on Jaguar and Daimler models.

Series III left-hand boot lid badge evolution, from top left. 1) Launch of Series III models brought a new Jaguar badge, later changed to a more prominent style; Daimler Sovereign models were similarly treated. 2) Daimler started to appear on the boot lid during Series III production. 3) Later Series III Jaguars used this engraved panel, with bold lettering style. 4) Revised design, with slender letters and new brushed finish, for very late Series III Jaguars.

Regardless of specification and name used, the same windscreen (laminated standard from June 1970) and rubber seal surround with inset bright trim (slimmer in cross-section from the end of 1970) and clips were fitted. Windscreen wipers were in chrome finish with anodised arms and chromed centre washer jets. The scuttle ventilator cover, positioned centrally between the wiper spindles, was initially also chrome-plated but in April 1970 this was changed to a satin bright silver finish to prevent glare; Series I and II VDP models had this scuttle vent painted body colour. In August of that year an expanded aluminium mesh filter was also added to the scuttle vent grille. The mesh was attached to the underside of the grille by the nut which also secured the windscreen washer jet assembly; it was recommended that this mesh was added to earlier cars when they returned to dealers for servicing.

Glass was supplied to Jaguar by Triplex and so marked, but in some cases the name Securiv Glass could be found on cars, either on all glass or certain panes only. There is no explanation for this other than shortage of supply or cost/trial changes. The option of clear glass, Sundym or Sundym with a shaded tint top area of the screen was available on all models at extra cost.

From the side all XJ6 and XJ12 cars were identical in body trim except for the long-wheelbase models, which featured elongated rear door window frames and glass. Although some small alterations were made to the internal workings of the door locks, the external handles remained unchanged during Series I production. Exterior door locks were fitted to both front doors and were of conventional style with a single-sided (FS) key. A key of different shape was used for the boot and glovebox locks and for the ignition.

All cars were fitted with a plain alloy tread plate to each door sill, attached by screws and also securing the sill carpet and Furflex trim. In October 1970 the Jaguar or Daimler name was incorporated in the centre section.

All Series I and II models should have an anodised trim finisher to the A-post water drain channel (visible when the front doors were open). Some, but not all, Series III models also have this.

Although no Series I Jaguars or Daimlers ever featured any swage coachlines, the upmarket Daimler Double-Six Vanden Plas had a chrome-plated trim with a curved face. This was used across both wings and doors following the body swage line. Each section of the chrome trim was entirely different so they are not interchangeable; for example the section on the front doors is cut away to accommodate the door lock. As a final finishing touch a hand-painted coachline, usually in gold (or charcoal where a contrast to the

Series I right-hand boot lid badge evolution, from top left. 1) The original style of 'litre' badging used on Series I models, here representing the 2.8. 2) Similarly the 4.2 litre style used on the Series I. 3) With the introduction of the V12 Series I, the XJ insignia appeared along with the number '12'; as there were now two wheelbase lengths, long-wheelbase models were also differentiated. 4) With export six-cylinder models and initially 4.2 litre cars for the home market, the XJ6 insignia only was used, again with an 'L' for long-wheelbase versions.

Series II right-hand boot lid badge evolution, from top left. 1) Engine sizes started to appear with the Series II models, Jaguars continuing with XJ lettering. 2) With Daimler Series II models only the 'litre' badge was shown on this side of the boot lid. 3) Coupé models had a 'C' within the boot badge. 4) On Daimler V12 models this style of 'Double-Six' badge – but not the Union flag! – was used to match the earlier Jaguar script on the opposite side of the lid.

Series III right-hand boot lid badge evolution, from top left. 1) Restyle of 'litre' badging and XJ insignia for Series III models. 2) New Vanden Plas badging moved to the right-hand side, with 'Daimler' now on the left instead. 3) Arrival of the more economical V12 HE power unit was shown off by Jaguar. 4) Introduction of Jaguar Sovereign models brought a new badge to match the Jaguar script on the left. 5) A new style of 'Double Six' badge (now without hyphen) appeared on later

Series III Daimlers. 6) The later style of Jaguar Sovereign badge was used alone on six-cylinder cars but a V12 motif always featured, initially of this style and aligned to the left. 7) Later the style and position of the 'V12' badge changed. 8) During the last year of production the Sovereign badge was discarded and a new V12 insignia was used, matching the brushed alloy finish and slender lettering style of the Jaguar badge.

Early Series I windscreen and rear screen chrome trims (far left) were large and flat in style. Thinner trims (left) were used on later Series I models, continuing for the Series II. Series III trims (below), showing their flatter appearance and new rubber sealing method.

exterior paint finish was required), was featured immediately below the swage line chrome.

The Vanden Plas was also fitted with a black vinyl roof which terminated at the front screen pillar top about 1in down (not at the base of the screen). At the rear the vinyl finished at the base of the rear pillar with a neat sculpted chrome finisher. Vanden Plas models were also fitted with a driver's door mirror, operated from inside the car. These were of the same type as used on later Series II and early XJ-S cars.

Doors and shut faces varied slightly. On most Series I models the courtesy light switches were unpainted galvanised metal, but black plastic was used for the last two years. A quite crude-looking bent piece of metal formed the child-proof lock switch on the shut face of the rear doors. Blanking plates fitted to the B/C post on the C post side were always galvanised and unpainted on all Series models. The door-shut catch plates were also galvanised and unpainted.

At the rear of the Series Is numerous changes took place over the years. All Jaguars featured a simplistic centrally-mounted chrome-plated boot lock with chromed surround, made up of two chrome-plated Mazak winged emblems bolted through the boot lid. On Daimlers, however, the winged emblems were replaced with a substantial chrome-plated Mazak surround, running the full width of the number plate, into which the central boot lock was fitted.

Number plates were normally fitted to a larger format than normal on British cars and were backed by four elongated rubber grommets that fixed through the boot lid. All number plates had a chromed surround with push-fit plastic clips through holes in the boot lid.

Lamp clusters were initially the same for all models. A wing-mounted cluster contained the rear lamps and indicators (different colourings to

The original finish on the scuttle ventilator for early Series I models was chromed (left), but later Series I and all Series II models had a satin finish (below left) to avoid glare. Body colour was used for Vanden Plas models.

Interior light courtesy switch evolution, from top left. 1) The metal type used on most Series I models, seen on the A-post. 2) The later black plastic switch used during the last two years of Series I production and into Series II models, again seen on the A-post. 3) On the B/C-post the switch (here the black plastic one) was always built into a galvanised face plate in natural finish. 4) Later Series II and early Series III plastic switch was white or ivory coloured. 5) Most Series III models used this type of switch throughout production.

The quite simple Jaguar treatment to the boot lock area and surround on the Series I models. Note also the Series I number plate illumination, incorporated in the bumper. Daimler models had a fluted full-width plinth that was very similar to the Series III style (see below), but shallower and retaining the 'winged' boot lock from the Jaguar version.

New boot finishers for Series II Jaguars (right) and Daimlers (far right) were of much deeper style, to accommodate number plate illumination

Series III boot finishers for Jaguars (right) and Daimlers (far right) had a separate boot lock, triggered by a chromed lever beneath the plinth.

suit export markets) and a long chrome-plated strip along the underside of the top edge of the boot lid contained reversing lamps and reflectors. This strip terminated in the middle at the chromed number plate surround.

Owing to changes in legislation, rear lighting treatment was altered on all cars from March 1970, although this did not seem to take effect until chassis numbers 1G.5048 (RHD) and 1G.52314 (LHD) on 2.8-litre cars, and 1L.6946 (RHD) and 1L.53570 (LHD) on 4.2-litre models. Reversing lamps were enlarged and reflectors were moved to a new position below the wing-mounted lamp clusters. Even the existing, and stylistically unaltered, stop/tail indicator lenses had to be altered to incorporate European lens markings from this date.

The rear bumper bar was made from one piece on early Series I cars but in March 1971 was changed to a three-piece unit to aid damage repairs. The two chromed side portions, which formed the wrap-around to the wings, met and interlocked with the straight centre section underneath the rear overriders. Within two years the old single-piece bumpers were no longer listed by the factory, so thereafter any damaged rear

bumpers were exchanged for the three-piece style in any case.

Number plate illumination on Series I cars was in the form of a rectangular unit, with chromed surround, mounted horizontally on the rear bumper and unchanged throughout production.

On the early cars nowhere would you find a Jaguar badge, only the engine size (either '2.8 litre' or '4.2 litre') in chrome on the right-hand rear face of the boot lid with the 'litre' wording as a separate badge below the engine size. Even the Daimler models initially did not feature a marque name, although the model name 'Sovereign' later appeared on the left-hand side of the boot lid, balancing the 'litre' wording. In contrast, cars for the US, where the 2.8-litre version was never offered, had the 'litre' script replaced with 'XJ6'. The Jaguar script returned for the US market in the form of a badge on the left-hand side of the boot lid to exactly the same style as used on the boot lids of Jaguar saloons in the '60s.

With the launch of the V12 came model identification on the right-hand side of the boot lid in the form of 'XJ' above and '12' below. For the Daimler equivalents a 'Double-Six' motif was used in the same position. With the launch of the Vanden Plas, this top-of-the-range Daimler also featured a scripted 'Vanden Plas' insignia to the rear left-hand side and the 'Double-Six' wording balancing it to the right as usual.

With the introduction of the long-wheelbase models in 1972, the cars were thereafter known as XJ6L and XJ12L; badging on the boot lid was altered accordingly.

Although radios were only fitted as an extra-cost option at this time (see *Optional Equipment & Accessories*, page 114), it is worth pointing out the positioning of exterior aerials on the Series I models. Initially a manual aerial was fitted on a front wing, usually on the driver's side, but due to design changes to the internals of the front wings this ceased to be possible. From mid-1969 the aerial was positioned on a rear wing, set well back near the extreme edge. However, some owners opted for a more expensive installation in the centre of the leading edge of the roof. Later all electric aerials were also sited on the rear wing.

While most Series II models had a rubber-finished bumper bar arrangement for North America, early cars for this market – and a few for other overseas markets – simply received rubber edging to the existing chromed bumpers.

All Series II V12 cars should carry this undertray, which is often discarded.

UK-specification under-bumper light units changed during Series II production, becoming all-amber, for indicators only, when the side lights were incorporated into the headlamps.

Vinyl roof details. Chromed rear wing finishers differ on Coupés (above right) and saloons (right). Front A-post view (below right) shows the point at which the vinyl should terminate, and also the overlap join along each side of the roof.

Series II

With the introduction of the Series II bodyshell came a host of detail external trim changes, many of which were brought about by legislation.

Starting from the front, legislation dictated raising the front bumper height. A wrap-around bumper of thinner section was used on European cars, while a rubber-faced impact-absorbing assembly (incorporating the number plate surround and indicators) was used on US models. In both cases a much shallower upper grille was featured, with a more prominent chromed surround matched to the bonnet shape. Jaguars used horizontal slats supported by four vertical slats, plus a prominent centre vane. V12-engined Jaguars also used the same grille but with a vertically-mounted badge on the centre vane, similar in layout to the Series I versions.

Daimlers, whether six-cylinder or V12 versions, used the traditional fluting to the chromed surround, which was even more prominent than on the Jaguars, with 13 vertical slats per side, separated by a single prominent centre vane. Centrally mounted at the top of the Daimler grille was the scripted 'D' emblem in silver against a black background or 'V12' in gold with the black background as before. As before, the shape of the grille blended with the Daimler central bonnet strip.

To compensate for the shallower radiator grille and to improve under-bonnet air flow, a new 'under-grille' ran the full length of the under-valance between the elongated 'underriders' leading upwards to stubby rubber-faced overriders on the bumper edges.

Headlamp treatment was unchanged from Series I cars, but new under-bumper indicator/sidelamp housings, made entirely from plastic, were fitted because of the raised bumper bar. From July 1978 all Series II models used a new style of headlamp incorporating the sidelamp unit, so the under-bumper unit served the indicators only, with the appropriate amber lens.

Number plates were again fitted to a black metal mounting, which in turn was bolted to the bumper (on chrome-bumpered cars), but the fixings were of simpler L-shaped metal.

In side view the Series II bodyshell looked the same as Series I models. However, a degree of hierarchy was established by judicious use of coachlines. For example, 3.4-litre models did not feature any coachline, 4.2-litre cars used a single coachline for most of the production run, and the V12 always had a coachline. These were finished to contrast with body colour, usually in gold, beige, red or black.

Daimler Vanden Plas models (both 4.2-litre and 5.3-litre) used the chromed swage line trims as on the Series I and also featured on the Daimler

Double-Six Coupé. Temporarily these trims also became standard on V12-engined Jaguar saloons and Coupés during the 1976 model year; thereafter they were deleted from all Jaguar versions.

The black vinyl roof obligatory on the Series II VDP cars, as on the Series Is, was now also fitted to all Coupé models, whether Jaguar or Daimler, although a much simpler, thinner chromed finisher was used where the vinyl met the rear wing. Also in a temporary vein, the roof covering was fitted to Series II V12-engined Jaguar saloons during the 1976 model year (with the VDP-style chromed side trims) and maintained for 1977 on the same models without the chromed trims.

Both front door locks were again of the same type as on the Series I models, except that now all door-operating keys were double-sided (FT type). For the Series II models the door courtesy light switches were of black plastic with chromed stops. On the last year of Series II production these changed to a white plastic finish.

At the rear exactly the number plate style was carried over from later Series I cars, although the number plate illumination now moved from the bumper bar to the chromed surround that also incorporated the boot lock. Narrower than the number plate but deeper to accommodate the lighting unit, this type was not repeated for the Daimler derivatives. Instead Daimlers used a more prominent fluted chromed unit which ran the full width of the number plate.

Badging on the Series II cars was both diverse and confusing. Initially the Jaguars always showed the Jaguar name to the left-hand side of the boot lid. To the right 'XJ' script of a new style was used, with the number '6' or '12' (with an 'L' for long-wheelbase models) beneath. On Coupés the letter 'C' was also included in the script. This situation changed on later cars, as the 'L' was dropped when

The two types of remote-controlled door mirror, for Series I/II (above) and Series III (left), the latter available with manual or electric adjustment.

Small trim items unique to Coupé models are the forward A-post finisher (right), the door rubber arrangement (centre right), and the B/C-post chromed and rubber finishers (far right).

the short-wheelbase bodyshells were no longer offered. Also from March of the last year of production, for European cars, the badging on six-cylinder models was changed to 'XJ 3.4' or 'XJ 4.2'. Simple XJ6 badging continued for the US market as the 3.4-litre model was not exported there.

On Daimlers a similar situation applied except that the word 'Sovereign' appeared instead of 'Jaguar' and the 'litre' mark '5.3' was replaced by 'Double-Six' as before. On Vanden Plas models a scripted 'Vanden Plas' appeared, staggered to the left-hand side of the boot lid, replacing the word 'Sovereign' as on the Series I cars.

Just to confuse, one other badge arrived when the V12 became fuel-injected in 1975. 'Fuel Injection' script was fixed to the left-hand side of the boot lid below the 'Jaguar' script or, in the case of Daimlers, 'Sovereign' script. This also applied to six-cylinder cars destined for the US and what is understood to have been a few right-hand drive examples produced just before the introduction of the Series III models.

Series III

With the launch of the Series III XJs came an entirely new bodyshell, although it retained much of the previous style.

Another new radiator grille was used, now of squarer format for the Jaguars and with only vertical slats for both marques. All Jaguar versions had a simple plastic centrally-mounted badge showing a silver 'growler' against a black background. In contrast, Daimlers retained the prominent profile of the Series II fluted grille with a centrally mounted badge with golden 'D' inset in a black background. The grille led to the usual central chromed bonnet strip. This strip, however, was deleted from all Daimlers from mid-1982,

necessitating a slight change to the shape of the radiator grille.

Headlamps had the same treatment as on previous models, and, dependent on model and age (see *Optional Equipment & Accessories*, page 114), a wash/wipe system was incorporated. From August 1979 flat-faced halogen headlamp units of a new style were fitted (Lucas H4). These were standard from then onwards on cars with wash/wipe, and were fitted retrospectively to earlier cars with wash/wipe. In January 1980 the headlamp rims were altered slightly to allow adjustment of the beams without removing the rims.

An entirely new bumper bar system was employed, both Jaguars and Daimlers using 5mph impact-absorbing buffers beneath a steel framework encased in moulded black rubber with chrome top fillets. The indicator lights, now rectangular, fitted into the moulded rubber bumpers and even the number plate had a moulded housing within the rubber. Beneath the bumper, the under-grille was now finished in matt black but with a chromed surround.

Larger front and rear screens were hermetically bonded to the car with new rubbers and flat-faced chrome trims and clips. Wipers now parked on the opposite side to previous Series saloons, and in June 1979 the driver's wiper arm was lengthened to 368mm (from 356mm) to improve the swept area. Wiper arms were initially bright finished, as on earlier Series, but from 1980 were finished in matt black anti-glare paint. The scuttle air intake was now chrome again and incorporated the screen washer jets.

Side indicator repeater lights were fitted to the outside edges of the wings and substantial remote-control, chrome-plated mirrors were fitted to both front doors. New chrome-plated door handles, set flush within matt black surrounds, were common

Series I/II door handle and lock treatment (below left) was the same except for the use of FT (double sided keys) on the Series II; chromed swage line strips for VDP and some other models required a cut-out to accommodate the lock barrel. Series III door handle and lock position differed (below right), later cars, as here, having the recesses powder-coated instead of painted to prevent the finish becoming chipped.

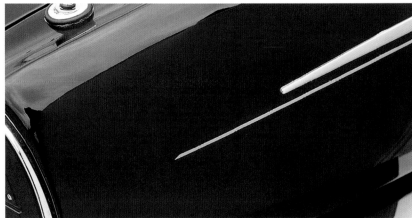

to all models. However, because of complaints about flaking paint, the black finish changed in January 1980 to a polyester powder coating. Repositioned door locks were of a totally different type from the Series II cars. Lastly, much larger window areas clearly identified Series III bodyshells.

The front side-mounted 'leaper' badges, which had been the same on all Series I, II and early Series III cars, were amended with the introduction of the Jaguar Sovereign models from 1983. They were now of a slightly rounded style with chrome surround and not handed. Daimlers had a scripted 'D'. Both marque badges were set against a black background.

As with some examples of the Series II models, Jaguar changed tack many times over exterior trim details according to model. For example, upon introduction of the Series III, the Vanden Plas models did not feature a vinyl roof or alloy wheels, instead using the same hub cap arrangement as on earlier models, adapted within 12 months to take stainless steel covers, as with Jaguars. It was not until the last few months of VDP production that Kent alloy wheels became standard on this model, and then only on 5.3-litre versions. VDPs did still feature the swage line chrome trims but these were now of flatter profile, without the cut-away on the front doors because lock position changed.

Courtesy light switches changed yet again with the Series III models, now having a black plastic finish with a nickel-type finish to the stops and switch surrounds. Series IIIs also featured

chrome-plated door lock faces. Child-proof locking now took the form of a push/pull nickel-finished rod with white plastic knob.

For 1982 through to 1983, non-VDP Daimlers were upgraded to create further differentiation from Jaguars. Externally this meant the use of chrome swage line trims from the VDP and new polished hub caps over the rimbellishers (these also ended up on some VDP models).

With the demise of the VDP models in 1983, the range of Daimlers was simplified to cover just 4.2-litre and 5.3-litre cars; all to the same basic external trim specification.

Coachlines moved around a lot on the Series III models. Initially 3.4s never featured a line, 4.2s a single coachline and 5.3s a twin line. By the introduction of the Jaguar Sovereign models in 1983, 3.4s and standard 4.2s were unchanged but a twin coachline appeared on all Sovereign models. Later that year even the 3.4-litre models got a single coachline. Coachline colour was gold, charcoal or black, normally to contrast with the body colour.

At the rear the same style of rubber-edged bumper bar was adopted. It incorporated high-intensity convex-style fog lamps in the rear straight section and rubber finishers to hide the join between the two side chromes and the rear straight. Interestingly, for certain export markets where rear fog lamps were not fitted, black rubber blanking plates could be substituted and were available for other markets upon request.

Lots of XJ models featured side coachlining (dependent on model year and type), but restorers often fail to achieve the correct start and finish points on the front and rear wings. These views show original coachlining with chromed swage line trim (black car) and without it (red car).

The same fuel filler cap (right) was used on Series I/II and most Series III models, but a much deeper design (far right) was fitted to catalyst-equipped Series IIIs. This extra depth accommodates a narrower filler neck (below right) that accepts only unleaded petrol pump nozzles.

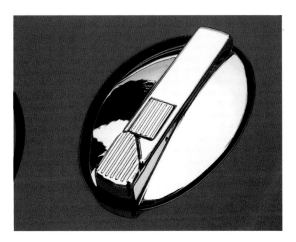

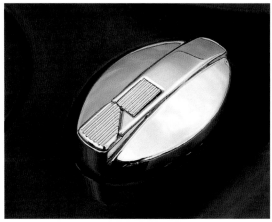

New lamp clusters incorporated all light and reflector units, thus allowing a cleaner approach to the rear of the boot lid. A simplified chromed boot surround of number plate width incorporated a new style of hidden boot lock mechanism and number plate lighting. This was smooth chrome for Jaguars and fluted for Daimlers. The number plate surround was still chromed.

Badging was amended yet again for the Series III models, with new script for the word 'Jaguar' on the left-hand side of the boot lid. To the right was new script again for 'XJ6' or 'XJ12'; on the former the 'litre' marking was also shown underneath as '3.4' or '4.2'. These badges were chromed plastic with a black shadow surround. For Daimlers a similar plastic treatment was used but the scripted 'Daimler' was found on the left, with '4.2', 'Double-Six' or 'Vanden Plas' on the right.

With the introduction of the high-efficiency version of the V12 engine, the 'HE' motif was used on all V12-engined saloons on the right-hand side. With the introduction of the Jaguar Sover-

eign models from 1983, the word Sovereign was also scripted to appear on the right-hand side of the boot lid above the 'litre' designation. Allied to this change came the demise of the Vanden Plas name from all European-market Daimlers and so a larger 'Double-Six' badge was used from then onwards. 'HE' badging was also dropped at this time. The Vanden Plas insignia remained in use for US market top-of-the-range Jaguars.

From 1985 all Jaguar badges were changed for rectangular chromed badges in embossed metal, with blackened script and border, the left-hand side of the boot lid depicting 'Jaguar' and the right-hand side 'Sovereign' plus '4.2' or 'V12' in the old open-style script. In 1986 the sill tread plates were changed for a highly polished stainless steel type with an embossed Jaguar or Daimler panel in the centre; this applied to all models.

For 1987 onwards, after the demise of the 4.2-litre Jaguar, the V12 Sovereign lost the name script but retained the 'V12' insignia in a rectangular brushed-aluminium badge to the right-hand side of the boot lid, with matching Jaguar badge on the opposite side. Similar treatment was also given to the Vanden Plas badging used on export Jaguars. Daimler badging remained unchanged through the remainder of production.

The only other change to trim came in February 1990, when engines were adapted to take unleaded fuel, which initially meant labels on the fuel fillers. Later came the use of a new-style filler with a narrower neck and deepened chromed filler cap to prevent the use of the larger leaded fuel pump nozzles. However, many cars from this time were not fitted with catalytic converters, which meant that the old-style fillers were still used.

This completes the detail changes to exterior trim on the Series I, II and III models. However, as detailed in the *Optional Equipment & Accessories* chapter (see page 114), many items were at the owner's discretion when ordering a new car, so it is possible that selected cars, which would not be so equipped normally, may have received vinyl roofs, alloy wheels, etc.

Boot & Tool Kit

The boot area on the XJ amounted to some 17cu ft of space with surprisingly few obstructions and a good, low loading area. On all Series the fuel tanks were hidden in the rear wings and the spare wheel, fuel piping and pumps were concealed beneath the boot floor in the spare wheel well or, in the case of the pumps, sometimes in the tanks themselves. Boot trim on the models changed many times over the period of production, although the general layout and configuration remained unchanged as this was part of the overall bodyshell design and altered very little over the three Series.

Series I

Upon the launch of the Series I Jaguars and Daimlers the boot trim area was finished in exactly the same way for both marques. The underside of the boot lid was a complex steel pressing with a cross-brace. The four triangular 'panels' created by the cross-bracing were filled with shaped black Hardura coverings glued into place. The boot lid on all models was counter-balanced by two substantial hinges, one at each corner at the rear of the lid. The underside of the boot lid and its hinges were always painted body colour.

An L-shaped panel covered the fuel pipes, which ran along the top edge at the rear of the boot (underneath the air extractor vents for the interior). This panel was painted black on Series I and II models.

The boot interior courtesy lamp was fitted to the underside of the lid and remained the same until the repositioning of the number plate lamp housing took place for Series II models. From then on, it was positioned in the centre of the lid itself (corresponding to the change in number plate illumination as detailed in the *Body Trim* chapter, page 34). At this time the boot interior lamp became part of that number plate lamp assembly. The automatic switch for boot lamp illumination was positioned to the right-hand rear area, by the hinge. On post-1970 cars this was switched in circuit with the sidelamps so that the light only operated when the sidelamps were on. The boot lid lighting wiring trailed from the rear offside

The Series I boot area with its plain Hardura matting, millboard side panels and black-painted L-shaped closing panel covering piping across the width of the car from hinge to hinge.

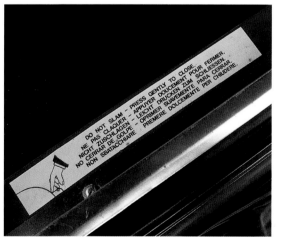

Series I models benefited from substantial sound-deadening underlay in the boot. Close-up shows boot closure warning label, applicable to all models and always fitted to the right of the boot catch.

Early Series I spare wheel installation showing the hinge and support bar for the hardboard cover, the very early press-formed fibre fuel pump cover and the correct type of spare wheel retaining clamp painted black.

Apart from very early examples of the Series I with a hinged spare wheel well cover in hardboard, all subsequent Series I and II models had a black-painted wooden cover secured at the rear by a lip.

(right-hand drive cars) of the bodyshell and entered the boot lid via the right-hand hinge, strapped to the side with nylon ties. This continued until the end of M-registered Series II models.

The boot surround was lined on three sides with millboard panels sprayed in a black matt finish and secured by Phillips self-tapping screws.

The boot floor covering was Hardura, again finished in black to match the underside of the boot lid and suitably bound. Initially the Hardura covering was a loose fit, but later it was secured by black-painted press-studs and shaped to match the flat floor area. At the rear of the boot a stepped section of flooring was necessary to clear the rear axle and this was also covered in black Hardura. A substantial under-mat sound-deadening panel of Hardura and felt, about 1in thick, was fitted.

The trailing edge of the boot area, where the boot lock was situated, was also stepped with elongated air extraction holes to allow free passage of air out of the boot. This was painted in body colour initially. An aluminium finishing panel was screwed to the leading edge of this panel and carried a warning label, printed in silver on red, advising owners not to slam the boot. All XJ Series boot lids should be pushed gently to locate the lock and not slammed.

Changes for Daimler Series I models included the use of black nylon boot carpeting instead of Hardura, and similarly carpeted side and back panels to replace the millboard from 1971. When introduced, V12 Jaguar and Daimler models had the carpeted boot area, whereas six-cylinder Jaguars retained the Hardura.

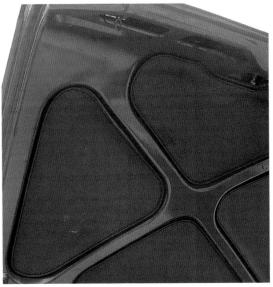

Underneath the boot floor trim was, initially, a bare hardboard panel with grip hole to cover the spare wheel compartment. The panel was held in place by a lip at the front and hinged to the bodywork at the rear with a support bar. During Series I production a plywood panel, painted matt black, was substituted and the rear hinge/stay arrangement was abandoned, a black-painted metal strip now being fitted to the back of the panel to aid location. In either case the panel was secured by two Dzus fasteners (one at each front corner) with an inset wing nut arrangement so the Hardura could lie flat on top.

The spare wheel well was always finished in body colour and unprotected. The spare wheel lay

Series I and early Series II boot lid underside, showing shaped Hardura panels, always black in colour, glued into position.

Electric cables leading into the boot were simply strapped to the driver's side boot hinge on Series I and earlier Series II models.

A relatively comprehensive tool roll of the same type was fitted to Series I and II models. The cars should have the correct named spanners to match the marque, but even the Jaguar factory could make mistakes – this original tool kit has a Daimler spanner mixed in with the Jaguar ones!

flat and was secured by different types of centre screw bolts according to Series.

Space was left at the front of the spare wheel to accommodate fuel pump arrangements for the majority of models, including petrol feed piping, fuel filters, etc. The types of pumps and fittings varied considerably through the model Series; for details on the various models see the *Carburettors & Fuel Injection* chapter (page 94). On Series I models the fuel pump area was covered by a pressed fibre casing painted matt black.

Series I models were not equipped with an elaborate tool kit, unlike many earlier and later cars, but instead an assortment modified from the then current E-type models. A pastel blue or grey wind-up jack with a fitting for the under-sill jacking points was supplied with a combined winding handle/wheelbrace (painted silver) in a black Hardura bag with tie strap. The bag rested on the spare wheel below the boot floor. Some batches of Series I cars from early to mid-1970 production were also fitted with a different design of grey jack. The tool kit itself, contained in a black Hardura-covered holdall, included a plug spanner with separate bar (usually black), black-handled screwdriver with interchangeable blades, black pliers, four open-ended spanners (all finished in black, with the Jaguar or Daimler name), chromed tyre pressure gauge, yellow plastic tyre valve remover, bright-finish feeler gauge and natural-finish metal hub cap remover. All spanners carried the 'Jaguar' or 'Daimler' name, as appropriate.

From April 1970 the shape of the fuel pump cover (made from wood and painted black) was changed and enlarged. This prevented the tools from being stored with the spare wheel, so a bracket was fitted in the left-hand side of the boot panelling to accept the tool bag.

The one-piece rubber boot seal style remained the same throughout production.

Series II

With the introduction of the Series II XJ models, very little altered in the boot area except that from 1976 the underside of the lid was clad in a single piece of millboard, painted black and secured with black press-studs. This remained the same for the rest of Series XJ production on all models. From 1976 all Series II models except the 3.4 received the black nylon boot coverings previously used for Daimler and V12 models.

On Series II models, the wooden cover for the

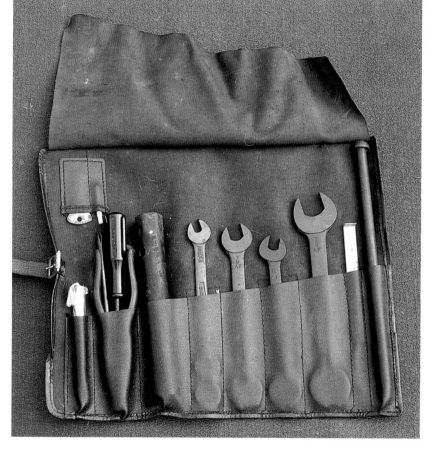

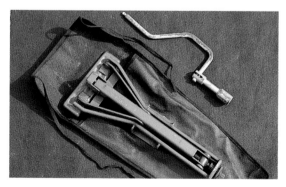

Two types of contemporary jack were used on Series I and II models. Most cars came with a blue jack (left), but a few had a grey one of totally different design (above). The tools seen with the blue jack are incorrect.

Later Series I and II six-cylinder Jaguar boot (right) still had a Hardura covering, but equivalent Daimler models and V12 Jaguars (far right) had a black nylon carpet and side coverings. Lack of space in the spare wheel well meant a new position for the tool kit and jack, removed in this case from the Daimler.

Series IIs gained compressed grey foam glued to the wooden spare wheel cover and fuel pump covers (right), a change that also applied to the very last Series Is, including VDPs. Under-floor view (far right) shows a revised spare wheel retaining clamp.

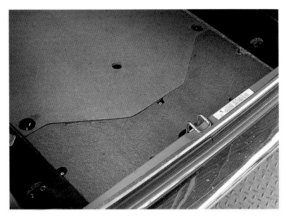 

Spare wheel well (right) applicable to both Series I and II models. The inspection panels, correctly painted black, were later abandoned for a full one-piece pressing as they served little purpose. Millboard fully covered the boot lid underside (far right) on later Series II and all Series III models.

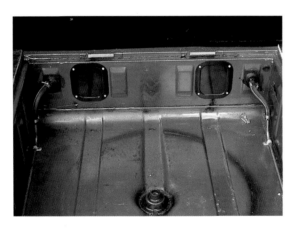 

Later Series II boot hinge on the driver's side with tidier electric cable arrangement (right), passing inside the hinge via a grommet. Boot closing panel (far right) on later Series II and III models received a fabric covering on cars equipped with nylon boot carpet.

Series III boot interior has better quality carpet with matching jack bag and a neat 'attaché' tool box. With carpet removed (far right), note the return to a square spare wheel well cover, another re-designed fuel pump cover and a single fastener for the spare wheel cover. Spare wheel well (below right) reveals another style of wheel clamp and a new steel well pressing.

petrol pumps within the spare wheel well was covered with grey ½in thick dense foam for sound insulation. This was applied to the whole boot floor area and was even glued to the cover for the spare wheel well.

At the same time lighting wiring in the boot lid was cleaned up and now entered a pre-drilled hole with black grommet in the right-hand hinge, eliminating the need for strapping.

Series III

With the introduction of the Series III models, a carpeted boot continued on all models. Side panels and rear bulkhead panels were also carpeted to match, in black or tan colour.

Jaguar reintroduced the age-old tool box for the Series III in the form of a black pre-formed plastic attaché case, which was strapped to the right-hand side panel. The case was badged 'Jaguar' or 'Daimler' according to model, fastened with a chromed toggle clip, and its hinged lip incorporated a handle. Inside, moulded slots held a good range of quality tools, which changed slightly, along with the layout within the case, around 1985. The tools included a wheelbrace, plug spanner with bar (later one-piece with uni-

When ABS braking was fitted to later Series III cars, the battery had to move to the boot, under its own cover. The boot also became slightly shorter due to the requirement to fit more electrics against the rear seat bulkhead (above). The boot closing panel (far right) was now an entirely new metal pressing with fabric covering.

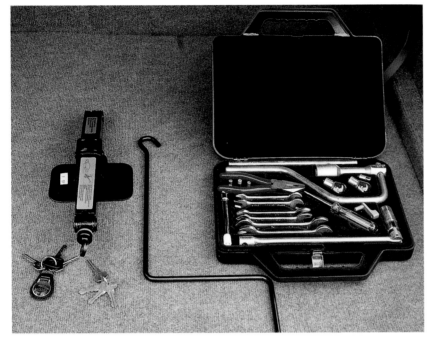

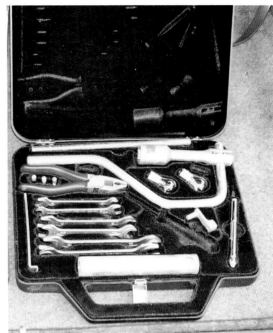

versal joint), pliers (red handle), a screwdriver (translucent yellow with interchangeable head), four spare bulbs, three spare fuses, six assorted open spanners, a tyre pressure gauge, feeler gauges, a handle to wind the sunroof (where fitted), and a hub cap remover (early on).

Two types of tool kit were fitted throughout production until 1991, when to standardise supply the larger XJ40 type of tool case was fitted with an appropriately larger strap to the right-hand side of the boot lid. The layout of the XJ40 tool kit was very similar to the earlier variety.

From October 1979 padding was fitted between the fuel pumps in the spare wheel well and the floor to cut down noise. A month later all cars were fitted with an extended boot courtesy lamp switch so that the light extinguished when the lid was a good 2in from closure.

Boot carpeting was rationalised from August 1982 for all models (except Jaguar and Daimler V12s) with the use of sisal boot floor carpet with PVC-coated felt and boot side panels in painted fibreboard. Daimlers received a new style double-sided boot carpet, black carpet to one side, black rubber to the other. From the introduction of the Jaguar Sovereign models in October 1983 all cars were standardised with full beige carpeting, with the jack in a similarly carpeted bag.

With the introduction of more sophisticated electronics and ABS from 1991 the rear bulkhead area of the boot was re-fitted, becoming slightly shallower to accommodate the equipment, but it remained carpeted in the usual way. The battery was relocated to this area, along with the various relays, etc. At this time Jaguar was recommending a Varta DIN 55 battery, which was located on the left-hand side of the boot, effectively under-

neath the rear window area. This type of battery, which had a translucent case for easy checking of electrolyte level, was recommended because the position made it difficult to check and fill a regular battery with distilled water.

A shaped cover in black grained plastic was held on to the battery carrier by two black, shaped fasteners. A vent pipe, supported on black metal stretchers, exited the boot compartment and was clipped to the rear subframe. The battery positive lead was the same as used on the XJ-S and was routed beneath the carpet along the transmission tunnel on the left-hand side. The negative lead went to an earth point in the boot. Battery clamp nut tightening torque was given as 25-30lb in.

The L-shaped panel covering the fuel pipes along the rear top edge of the boot was changed on Series III models to metal with a figured black vinyl finish.

Different styles of 'attaché' tool case for Series III models, the later type (above left) differing from the earlier one (above right) in tool details.

Attaché cases carried the 'Jaguar' or 'Daimler' logos as necessary, while the last Series III V12 models were equipped with the more compact XJ40 tool case without a handle, seen with the earlier type Daimler-badged case.

Interior Trim

The essence of the interior trim of all Series XJ Jaguars was one of quality and ambience, although many of the materials did not always match up to this quality image. Also some of the materials used are not that readily available today. Changes were significant not only by Series but also by model and actual year of manufacture, so again we must take each Series separately. Daimler aspects are identical unless otherwise stated.

Series I

Woodwork

The original Series I cars and all later derivatives featured the traditional theme of walnut veneer for the dashboard and some allied areas. The dashboard itself on Series I models was of conventional composite wood with a walnut veneer glued into place. Some matching of veneers did take place although not to the standard of traditional coach-built cars. The figuring of the veneer did not vary between Jaguar and Daimler models, except for the Vanden Plas (see below).

The only hint of other woodwork on Series I Jaguar models was in the door cappings. A simple stained and polished sliver of wood was attached to the top of each door trim by chrome-plated Phillips screws with cup washers. This was a little more complex on the rear doors where the flat capping lifted to form a more substantial style at the base of each rear quarterlight.

With the introduction of the Daimler models the dashboard treatment remained unaltered and, surprisingly for this up-market marque, the door cappings were eliminated in favour of an entirely new door trim (see below).

The Vanden Plas Series I model was treated differently and the veneering was of superior quality throughout production, with improved matching and figuring. Dashboard outer panels incorporated boxwood inlay that curved upwards at each end to match the shape of the panel.

Wooden fillets with boxwood inlays were also incorporated in all four door trims, a reasonably substantial thickness of wood as can be identified by the detail finishing of the panels wrapped around to the door edges – a nice quality touch.

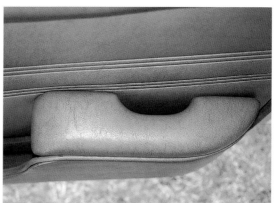

Door Trim Panels

Door trim panels were of board construction with Ambla padded coverings to match the interior colour scheme. On Jaguar six-cylinder models three sets of three horizontal heat-embossed ribs were featured to break up the plain panels, and extra padding was shaped around the recessed chrome-plated door handles and at the top of the trims where the cappings were attached. Armrests on the front doors were shaped to include a handy pocket upholstered in felt. In 1970 these armrests were redesigned to include a finger grip to aid closure of the doors.

Front door trim style for the Series I XJ6. This car has electric windows, with operating buttons situated on the centre console rather than the door. Later Series I models received a revised armrest (left) with door pull grip. On Series I Jaguar and Daimler models, front quarterlight (below) was operated by a knurled knob – an idea stolen from Mercedes cars!

Series I XJ6 rear door trim, again with electric windows. Rear window controls were mounted within the door pocket (above), which had a trim-coloured felt inlay at the bottom.

Door trim treatment on Series I Daimler models and subsequent V12 Jaguars, seen on front (right) and rear (far right) doors – although V12 Jaguars did not feature the chrome trim at the top.

Vanden Plas Series I and II models had different door trim treatment reminiscent of later Series III styles (see page 56). Woodwork was substantial and terminated abruptly, as if to show it off! Note the boxwood inlay used on VDP models.

On the rear doors a much more horizontal and substantial armrest and pocket was used. Note that on the listed 'Standard' models door armrests and pockets were not featured. With the introduction of Daimler and long-wheelbase models, the door trims, although still of the same padded material, were much plainer, without any embossing. The front door pockets were longer and more shapely, with the armrest/door pull sweeping up to meet the door release. This provided a much deeper oddments pocket and enabled door-mounted speakers for audio equipment to be fitted more easily. The rear door pockets on Daimler

models were inset too, with trim-coloured felt like the front but on Jaguars a pre-formed black plastic insert was fitted.

To lift the rather plain look of the door panels, Daimler models gained a black vinyl covering to the top section, with a substantial horizontal chrome strip running the full width of each door.

On all these models carpeting to match the interior was fitted at the bottom of the front door panels as a protection against scuff marks, and there was also a chrome finisher.

For the Vanden Plas model door trims were again different. Firstly, although retaining the blackened top section used on the other Daimlers, the Vanden Plas had a full-width veneered wooden fillet instead of a chrome strip. Door pockets were entirely different, completely separate from the armrests, and they also contained the four matching speakers for the stereo system. The whole of the door trims were leather on this model. The armrests were substantial and sloped back towards the rear of each door. Interestingly this treatment for armrests and door pockets was to be used on later Series Jaguars and Daimlers. Another fitting on VDP models was the adoption of small circular red warning lamps, with a chromed surround, in the end sections of all four

With the Vanden Plas models came a red warning light in the rear face of each door. The finish was initially chromed, but later, when these lights were also fitted to Sovereign Series III models, the finish became black.

doors. The lamps illuminated automatically when a door was opened as a warning to other road users.

Door furniture was made up of the recessed chromed release levers with vertically ribbed, chromed back plates and 'flip' levers to lock the doors from the inside. Where manually operated windows were specified, the winders were chromed with black plastic knob surrounds. The correct positioning for the window winders with the windows fully closed is with the arm vertical (knob to the bottom). A knurled black plastic knob with a chromed centre operated the front door quarterlights.

Where electric windows were fitted, the switch pack for the front doors was situated on the centre console, but for the rear doors there was a substantial chromed control inside each door armrest. VDPs used an enlarged rear section of the centre armrest to accommodate the switches.

Ambla trim was continued for the B/C post covering, with extensive use of Furflex around the four door-frame edges in the same colour as the seat trim. Sill tread plates were made of aluminium, patterned on the early cars and held in place by two self-tapping screws in the rear compartment and four on the front sills. See *Body Trim* (page 28) for details of sill tread plate changes.

The same 'Daimler' treatment was given to the Jaguar XJ12 except for the black trim, XJ6 wooden cappings being used instead.

In any of the above models fitted with radio/cassette systems, speakers would have been inset into the bottom forward section of the door trims accordingly.

Seats

Jaguar seats for six-cylinder and V12 models were identical, with Slumberland springing and leather facings, the then fashionable perforated upholstery supposedly allowing air to circulate around the seat and body area. The style, with ten pleats for each front seat section and 17 in the rear, did not vary with Jaguar models. On the 2.8-litre 'Standard' model all upholstery was Ambla, with no leather content at all. Front seat backs were a mixture; the top section was plain but the lower area was a pre-formed fibre panel, nylon-covered

to match trim colour, with two embossed borders.

Early cars had no provision for head restraints in the front seats, but from August 1969 head restraint fittings were supplied as standard, with a chrome surround and plastic finisher in black. Head restraints were an extra-cost option on all Jaguar and Daimler Series I models except for the Vanden Plas.

Daimler models used the same seat frame but slightly fuller padding and wholly non-perforated leather covering with wider pleats (five to each

The style of front seating used on Series I and II Jaguar models, with aerated leather pleating.

General view shows the nylon-covered seat backs of Series I and II Jaguars. This early Series I has no facility to fit head restraints, but later Series I models received blanked-off sockets (right) to enable extra-cost head restraints to be fitted.

front section, seven for the rear). Front seat backs were plain Ambla on Daimlers. On V12 models seat pleating was as per Jaguar or Daimler styles.

Where head restraints were fitted, these were of the plain or perforated leather type, dependent on Jaguar or Daimler trim style, and in some cases were of Ambla instead of leather.

Vanden Plas models were different again, with less sculpting to the seats and only four wide pleats in each section, front and rear. VDPs also gained map pockets in the rear of the front seats, all fin-

ished in leather, and were equipped with leather-covered head restraints as standard equipment at the front. These were of a more substantial style and fit than on other models.

All seats at this stage were manually adjustable for combined reach and height by a spring-loaded bar at the underside front of each seat. The bars were painted black on Jaguar Series I and II, chromed for Daimler and Vanden Plas models. All Series I front seats had reclining mechanisms operated by a chrome-plated handle to the door side of each seat. A millboard finisher, in the upholstery colour with an anodised trim surround, hid the mechanism.

Rear seat shape and style was initially the same on all models, except for the 'Standard' 2.8-litre model, on which no centre fold-down armrest was fitted. Jaguar and Daimlers altered only according to pleat style except for the centre armrest, which was smaller but deeper on Daimlers. Rear head restraints were never fitted to Series I models.

The Vanden Plas rekindled a previous trend for Jaguar with the Mark VIII and IX saloons of the late '50s, and had a separately sculpted rear seat with a more prominent centre armrest.

Seat belts were not standard equipment on Series I models, except for the Vanden Plas which

Daimler Series I front seating (left), with unperforated leather and broader pleats than on Jaguar versions. Compared with Jaguar models, Daimler Series I and II rear compartment (above) shows different backs to the front seats, broader pleats and a different centre armrest.

Rear seating of Series I XJ6 and XJ12 Jaguar models was carried over to the Series II cars (below). Jaguar style of centre armrest can be seen.

Another style of seating was reserved for Series I and II Vanden Plas models. Pleating is different again, and rear seats have an 'individual' design, separated by a very large armrest.

had front inertia reel Kangol units encased in externally-mounted silver grey coloured mechanisms attached to the sills through the carpets. These belts carried the 'D' insignia on the buckles. Where belts were specified on other models, they tended to be of the lap and diagonal type, again of Kangol make, and secured to pre-fitted mountings in the tops of the B/C posts below the courtesy lamps. All seat belts at this stage would have been finished in plain black or charcoal colour and not in the trim colour.

Centre Consoles & Carpets

Consoles were upholstered in Ambla to the same style and shape on all cars except VDPs. The trim covering joined in the centre of the top of the console, the join covered with a fillet of trim-coloured fibreboard. Secondary 'cheek' panels, also trimmed in Ambla (or carpet on VDPs), were attached to the side of the console to hide various aspects of the heating system (and air conditioning where fitted). These panels were held in place by self-tapping chromed screws, cup washers and underside clips. Switchgear details are covered in the *Facia & Instruments* chapter (page 62).

The armrest itself formed a rear-hinged section which lifted at the front to reveal a glovebox area with black pre-formed board insert, the outer edge forming part of the alloy trim. On Daimler models a flock pad insert was glued to the base. The 2.8-litre 'Standard' XJ6 made do with a simple open storage tray.

For the benefit of rear seat passengers, an air flow extractor swivel vent with switching was fitted at the rear of the armrest/console. The vent was chromed on early cars and later changed to a black plastic finish in line with changes to instrumentation (see page 62). This did not apply to 'Standard' models, which did not have a heating and ventilation system fitted. For those models a simple ribbed alloy panel filled the space. A third ashtray, of exactly the same type as used at the front, was fitted for the benefit of the rear passengers. Finally the rear of the console was secured through the carpet to the floorpan by two chromed self-tapping screws (one either side).

Two distinct types of chromed ashtray were used. The Series I and II ashtray had a sharp lip edge to the lid and the insert had two elongated holes through which ash and waste paper could be passed. For Series III models the lid gained a curved lip without the sharp edge, and the insert had only one lengthened hole for ash and waste. In all cases correct fitting for console-mounted ashtrays is to have the lid closing inwards (towards the gear shift).

All Series I cars (except for the very first few off the production line) had two under-dashboard oddment shelves, one each side. Of millboard construction with a padded black surround in vinyl and black flock covering on the face side, they were shaped at the corners nearest the doors.

Carpets on all models were of an identical nylon type (except for the VDP with a deeper pile Wilton) edged in vinyl and matched to upholstery colour. Carpets were secured front and rear by black press studs. Sound-deadening material below the carpet was black-covered ½in thick underfelt, cut to the size and shape of each footwell. Cut strips of multi-coloured condensed rubber were positioned between the floorpan indentations beneath the underfelt. Both front footwells contained an inset rectangular PVC heel pad to protect the carpet from wear. Carpeted areas around the inner sills and on the rear seat pan area were shaped, fitted and glued in place.

Headlining & Fittings

The headlining on all Series I XJs was of the pre-formed type made from glass-fibre board with a covering of foam-backed nylon glued to it. The

Carpet style on the Series I XJ models. As on the driver's side, the passenger side also has a heel pad. Note the stitched-in binding; black stud fasteners are not correct on this car.

Extensive sound-proofing insulation was fitted beneath Series I carpets. Hardura was glued to the floorpan, then multi-coloured compressed foam strips were inserted into each strengthener pressing to create a flat surface for underlay and carpet.

board was pressed into position as a composite with the headlining, which was finished in beige, tan or grey. The finished headlining assembly was secured in position by wooden battens, padded and covered in the same material, clipped into a wooden roof surround with black push-clips.

The sun visors were fitted on the battening around the top of the windscreen. The two visors were entirely separate and finished in plain, padded, heat-seamed, black vinyl. These visors were secured to the batten at each far corner (nearest the doors) by chromed swivel bars and sockets, each held in place by three chromed screws. Neither sun visor had a pocket or vanity mirror at this time.

The rear-view mirror was fitted to the centre of this screen batten by a triangular attachment with chromed screws. The mirror was designed to

Close-up showing head-lining texture and chromed coat hook fitted in the rear of all Jaguar versions plus Daimler 3.4 litre models.

Sill kick plates on early Series I cars were plain, but later Series Is had this ribbed style incorporating the marque name which continued throughout Series II and into early Series III production.

This headlining style was used throughout Series I and II production. Note black sun visors and padded bolster finishers around the sides above the door frames.

snap off in an accident and originally had a chromed stem and a ribbed aluminium back panel. This was changed from May 1970 for a satin-finished stem with black mirror back. All rear-view mirrors could be dipped, by means of a white plastic 'ball' just below the centre.

The rear parcel shelf was finished in black Ambla with a raised centre section (also trimmed) to allow air extraction. This section was strengthened in 1970 after complaints of heat damage, and a few cars received vertical black plastic 'supports' in an attempt to stop oddments and papers sliding

along the shelf when driving through corners.

Where a radio was installed, it was recommended that the rear speaker should be sited to the offside (on right-hand drive cars) of the parcel shelf with a rectangular bronzed grille. Where a stereo unit was specified, as on the Vanden Plas, speakers would be fitted in the rear door trims.

The parcel shelf on Vanden Plas Double-Six models was entirely different, having a shaped and more prominent centre extractor vent. The whole shelf was finished in the interior trim colour, much to the same style as the later Series III cars.

Interior lighting took the form of one defused white light per side on the B/C post at roof height.

For the Daimler models, rear passengers had the benefit of grab handles, finished to match the interior with chromed fixings and movable chromed coat hooks. Each grab handle was fixed centrally above each door on the battened area.

VDP cars were also equipped with rear compartment reading lamps. A beautifully designed swivel-jointed lamp in chromed finish was fixed by chromed screws to each rear quarter batten directly above the door quarterlight glass. The light would come on automatically when the lens was swivelled downwards.

Series II

With the introduction of the Series II came a new approach for Jaguar, one very much geared to safety and ergonomics Hence there was a totally new dashboard (described in the next chapter) and the elimination of all sharp edges and extensive use of padding.

Woodwork

There was less wood in the Jaguar and Daimler Series II, save for the Vanden Plas models. The only wood was on the facia panel, which was a continuation of the same theme as on the Series I except for the layout. The Vanden Plas again benefited from better quality veneer in general and retained the door cappings with double boxwood inlay, although this inlay was dropped from the dashboard areas.

Door Trim Panels

The front door trims were of a new style and if anything a composite of the later Jaguar and Daimler Series I models. The armrest was altered in style but still swept up to meet the door release lever. The door pockets, however, were enlarged after complaints from owners that the Series I door pockets were not of much use. Added for the Series II was a carpeted panel with chrome finisher, as on the earlier Daimlers.

Gone were the wood fillet cappings, replaced with vinyl trim as an integral part of the panel but

with another chrome finisher across the entire width of each door. The vinyl trim above the chrome finisher was trim colour on Jaguars and all 3.4-litre cars, but still black on 4.2-litre and 5.3-litre Daimlers. Cars with nylon upholstery also had door trims in nylon, although the trim above the chrome finisher remained vinyl. Under this, heat embossing returned in the form of two shaped lines joined to form an elongated five-sided shape.

The same layout was carried over for the longer doors of the Coupé models, incorporating longer armrests and door pockets accordingly.

Similar treatment was used on the rear doors but the pocket remained as on Series I Jaguar/Daimler models. The existing door lever and back plate arrangement was used but beneath this on the rear doors was a chromed pull-out ashtray with black padded inset. These door-mounted ashtrays replaced the centrally-mounted one at the rear of the console because of the use of electric windows on many models (see below).

For the Coupé the rear panel treatment was very different and the pocket formed part of the trim leading to the back seat. The armrest also had to be altered but the general shaping, embossing, etc, remained unchanged.

For the 3.4-litre cars the door panels were entirely plain, without any embossing at all. From

Revised door trim treatment at front (top left) and rear (top right) for Series II Jaguar four-door saloons, and likewise at front (above left) and rear (above right) for Daimler models. While Daimler models in the main continued with a felt insert for the rear door pockets, Jaguars got a pre-formed fibreboard inlay in black (left). This was also fitted to other models where radio speakers were accommodated in the rear doors.

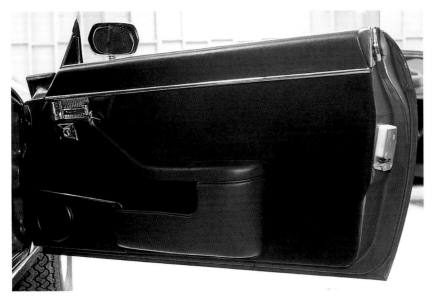

Door trims of the Series II 3.4-litre model at front (top left) and rear (top right). Door trim on the Coupé (above), this being a nylon-upholstered example with nylon therefore used on the door panels as well.

the 1977 model year all Series II models except VDP cars used the same style of plain finish for the door trims.

Series II VDP models were exactly the same in this department as on the Series I models, apart from changes to colour schemes. When remote-control exterior door mirrors (standard on VDPs, optional on other cars) were fitted, the control unit was a rectangular chromed panel screwed to the door trim. The position of this had to be changed on Coupé models because of the lack of a fixed quarterlight.

All materials used, including door furniture, were the same as on Series I cars.

Seats

Front and rear perforated seating with narrow pleats for the Jaguar models was exactly as found on the Series I cars, although colour schemes altered (see page 122). Daimlers still had wider pleats (five in each front seat, seven in each rear

section) and smooth leather without perforations. On most Series II models head restraints were standard, but still only on the front seats. They were finished in leather (or occasionally for some reason in Ambla) to match upholstery colour.

On the 3.4-litre Series II saloon cloth seats were standard instead of leather, although the style and number of pleats were unchanged. Front seat adjusters were of exactly the same type as on Series Is but now the chromed finish applied to all Coupés and V12-engined cars as well. Head restraints were also not fitted to 3.4-litre models. It should be noted that many 3.4-litre cars were supplied to special order with leather upholstery, and that some other models were also specified at time of build with cloth trim.

For the two-door Coupé models the seats were initially the same as the saloon although the front seat backs were plain and folded forwards to allow better access to the rear seats. The backrest was released by a black triangular-shaped lever mounted on a chromed panel on the outside edge. On all Series II models the board finisher to the recliner was as on Series Is, but with nylon upholstery this was also finished in nylon. The Coupé rear seat was of the same design as on the saloons but obviously cut down slightly in size and shape.

Vanden Plas models retained the same seating arrangement as on the Series I cars.

For the 1976 model year the top-of-the-range Jaguar V12-engined cars and all Coupés received the benefit of Daimler-style leather upholstery with plusher, wider pleats, without perforations. Other models with leather trim retained the older style of upholstery.

Centre Consoles & Carpets

Again the general arrangement and materials were the same on Series IIs as on Series I models. However, the carpets were of a new nylon weave

Rear seating in the XJ Coupé, in this case a nylon-trimmed car.

of a poorer quality and a new range of colour schemes was used (see page 122). Underlay was of a similar style to Series I models but the underlay strips on the floorpan were of black rubber, which continued for the rest of Series XJ production.

Vanden Plas models gained a new Birstall Evlan Wilton style of deep-pile carpet throughout and loose long-pile nylon 'over-rugs' for the front and rear passengers. Underfelt was also much deeper to keep noise levels down on VDP models.

The centre console was also of exactly the same layout at the front, although now, with the new heating and air conditioning system, the side 'cheeks' contained ventilators as described in the *Facia & Instruments* chapter (see page 69). The centre console box area was also the same except that now the surround was finished in black and not alloy as previously. At the rear of the console the layout was also the same except that, on the majority of cars equipped with electric windows, the two window rocker switches (the same style as the front switches) were located here, replacing the ashtray.

For VDP models the rear console protruded further along the transmission tunnel to allow space for the retention of the Series I style chromed ashtray. Also a cigar lighter for the rear passengers was fitted between the window-lift rocker switches.

Headlining & Fittings

Again these were of exactly the same style, layout and materials as used on the Series I cars. Daimlers, as before, were fitted with grab handles in the

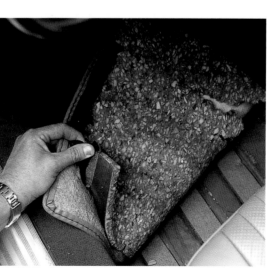

Front carpet style did not change for the Series II models, but the size of the heel pad increased. Under-carpet treatment differed from the Series I in using multi-coloured compressed foam for the underlay and black rubber strips to fill in the strengthener pressings.

Earlier woollen and nylon 'over-rugs' fitted initially only to Vanden Plas models.

rear roof area above the doors, except for the 3.4-litre Sovereign which only got a chromed coat hook in the same position, as also applied to all Jaguar models. VDPs also had an extra grab handle on the batten over the front passenger door, although in this case without coat hook. All grab handles were now finished in black and not trim colour.

Coupés used a different headlining arrangement, which incorporated special interior light units with a magnifier section. Two grab handles were also added to the Coupé specification as on the Daimler four-door models.

Seat belts were a standard fitting by this time. Simple lap and diagonal types were fitted to all cars except the Vanden Plas models. Belts were always finished in black, with anchorage points on the B/C posts on saloons and in the top trim section of the rear wing panels on Coupés.

Sun visors were as on Series I models until the last year of Series II production, when a simpler swivel-action fastening was adopted, with 'parking' clips to hold the revised visors in the upright position.

Sun visor fixing on Series I and early Series II models used a chromed ball joint (right). Simpler arrangement for later Series II models (below)

had a black fixing allowing the visor 'rod' to swivel, and black clips now secured the visor in the normal position.

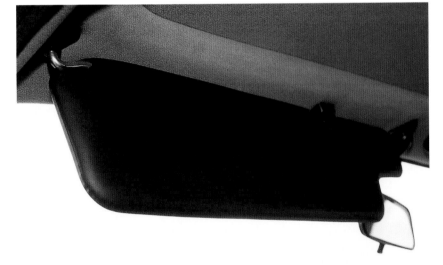

Series III

The introduction of the Series III models brought with them much the same interior features, but with many differences in detail. Most of the trim changes were subtle but enhanced the traditional feel of luxury associated with the XJ range of cars.

Woodwork

The style and content of woodwork was unaltered on the early Series III models. Changes only started to take place from the 1981 model year, when Daimlers received the VDP-style walnut veneer cappings to the top door trims. These were added to the Jaguar Sovereign on its introduction for the 1984 model year. However, door cappings on all Series III models were not of the same quality as earlier VDP cars. The wood formed a thin sliver inset into the padded door trim.

From the autumn of 1985 all cars were then fitted with the door capping woodwork regardless of model. From then, however, only the Daimler Double-Six models carried the boxwood inlay as standard. All cars also gained a veneered centre console section.

Also from 1985, Jaguar introduced a new style

Combined coat hooks with black/chrome hand pulls were standard on Daimler models and all Coupés; on Vanden Plas Series I models the hand pull matched trim colour.

This Coupé view also shows the model's revised interior lighting, necessary because there was no B/C-post to carry the conventional saloon interior light.

The style of trim used on the door panels of earlier Series III models (above). Later Sovereign and Daimler style on Series III models is seen on front (right) and rear (below right) doors.

of straight-grain veneer on the 3.4-litre model. This finish was carried over to the door cappings and centre console for this model only, and remained standard until the end of production.

Door Trim Panels

Again there were no changes from Series II, except for the standard fit of door-mounted speaker grilles, circular and black finished. At the rear these were mounted within the door pocket area with suitable trim concealing the interior.

Cars equipped with remote-control exterior mirrors used a different style of switch-pack on the very early Series III cars. Chromed and inset into the door trim (above the chrome strip), this switch-pack was not deeply set into the back plate as on Series II cars, and had black button joysticks. For the 1981 model year the switch-pack was changed to the later style with chrome joystick buttons and angled back plate. Daimlers at this stage received this feature on both front doors as standard equipment. From 1991 the switch-pack changed again for a simple multi-functional black plastic round knob on a ball and socket arrangement set into the front door pocket trim.

All cars produced after September 1980 received new speaker shrouds on the door trims to protect them from water running down the inside of the door casings.

At the 1981 model year all Series III models received the circular red warning lamps in the doors previously seen only on the Series II VDP models. The surrounds of these lamps were now black, not chrome. At the same time, for Daimler models only, red 'puddle' lamps, which illuminated when opening a door, were fitted at the rear of each door armrest. This feature was also standardised on Jaguar Sovereign models from their introduction, and then on all models from the end of 1985.

From August 1982 twin electrically controlled

door mirrors became standard on all V12 cars and optional on others until 1985, when they were applied to all models. At the same time the finish of the door release lever back plates changed from chrome to black.

At the introduction of the Jaguar Sovereign

Three different styles of remote door mirror control used on Series III models.

Mid-term Series III Jaguar front seats (right) saw the return of perforated upholstery. Subtly different styling for the Vanden Plas (far right) subsequently became standard on all later Daimler Series III models. Note electric adjustment for seat height and chromed fore/aft movement bar (the Jaguar bar was black).

Front seat back used on VDP Series I/II/III models, plus later Series III Daimlers equipped with VDP-style seats.

Detail of hand stitching used on Daimler models in the Vanden Plas Series I/II/III, plus other Daimler Series III models.

models for the 1984 model year, these cars regained the black treatment to the upper door trim panel above the chrome strip line and exactly the same door pocket/armrest style as the previous Vanden Plas models. With this trim panel change, the controls for the remote control door

mirrors moved to the top front section of the door pocket trim. Other models at this time (without the wooden fillet door capping) remained in matching trim colour, and in fact even when the wooden fillets were added at the end of 1985 the pocket/armrest style remained unchanged.

Seats

Seat style was similar to the later Series II models, but with wider pleats (five at the front) and non-perforated upholstery. On the rear seat, however, the number of pleats was standardised with eight. More 'plushness' was given to all seating with the addition of extra filling to provide stiffer bolstering. Seating was finished in leather for all models except the 3.4-litre Jaguar, which had cloth upholstery; this could still be specified as a no-cost option on other models.

Lumbar support for both front seats was now provided in the form of a revolving drum within the seat to effectively harden the backrest. This was operated by a three-eared black plastic control on the inside edge of the backrest.

Similarly some models gained electric adjustment for the front seat cushion. An electric motor underneath the seat raised or lowered the rear of the cushion. The switch, a black rectangular 'flipper' in a chromed surround, was positioned to the front side of the base of the seat. Standard from the start on the VDP model, where it was fitted to both front seats, this seat adjustment became standard on all Daimler models from August 1982 but

remained optional on Jaguars. From January 1980 all seat stitching was in trim colour to improve aesthetics.

For the 1981 model year, coinciding with changes to the steering wheel style (see *Facia & Instruments*, page 68), perforated upholstery made a comeback on Jaguar models with leather trim. The wider pleats were retained and the perforations were of a more closely-knit type compared with the earlier cars. At the same time Daimler models gained the rear seat head restraints introduced on the first of the Series III Vanden Plas models. These were standard now on all Daimlers and optional on Jaguars.

From August 1982 all cushioning was revised, with substantially improved diaphragms to stiffen the seating and provide more lateral support. For non-leather cars a new style of closely-knit, smoother polyester cloth was used, with very wide three-pleat stitching on the front seats and five pleats per section at the rear. For the 1983 model year the material changed to a new soft woven velour (Rachelle cloth) with featured ribbing. This type of cloth upholstery remained in use until November 1985, when 3.4-litre models received a new herringbone-pattern wool tweed. This was also available as a no-cost option on other models, but only to special order.

Individually sculpted rear seats with flatter pleating at the front were introduced on non-VDP V12 Daimlers in November 1985. A new-style bench seat, with the same flatter form as the front VDP style and seven pleats per section, could be specified at no extra cost on Daimlers. The sculpted rear seating also benefited from a change to slightly thinner pleats.

The centre armrest on the VDP rear seat remained unchanged and would be carried forward to non-VDP models after the demise of the use of the name on the UK market. For Daimlers fitted with the alternative new-style bench seat, the centre armrest did not open.

From 1985 contrast-colour piping became an option on leather-clad cars.

The later slightly revised style of VDP seating for the Series III, also adopted for all later Daimlers. This sculpted look for the rear parcel shelf air extractor in the centre is much more elaborate on VDP models and the majority of Series III models.

Jaguar seating remained relatively constant on Series III models. Note on this later car (above and left), without perforated upholstery, the style of pocket in each front seat back, and the standard fitting now of head restraints on all seats. To special order Daimler owners could specify a rear bench (right) instead of the normal 'individual' seating.

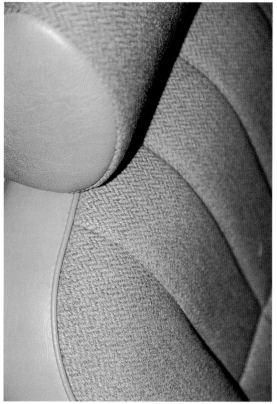

Two of the types of non-leather seat facings found in Series III Jaguars. Ribbed Rachelle cloth (far left) was used until the onset of a wool-blend tweed style (left).

Centre Consoles & Carpets

A new sandwich of sound-deadening material was laid on the floorpan under the carpet. The same style and structure of carpet was used as on Series II models, made up of ½in foam and ³⁄₁₆in of lining.

For 1981 all Daimlers gained the nylon 'over-rug' treatment previously only available on VDP models. For the same model year all Daimlers now received the Vanden Plas style of central console, with the rear incorporating the extra cigar lighter, but with a completely black vinyl backing replacing the previous alloy finish.

In the same year the driver's carpet heel panel insert was changed to rubber, colour-coded to the upholstery and now incorporating the Jaguar or Daimler emblems according to marque. From August 1983 the carpet in the front compartment was extended to meet the A-post at sill level, covering an area that was previously vinyl trimmed.

With the introduction of the Jaguar Sovereign models, the centre console received a revised upward section where it met the dashboard (see *Facia & Instruments*, page 71). The surrounding Ambla trim was always black on Jaguars, but on Daimler V12s it was finished in other interior trim colours to match the seats. However, a few of the very last V12 Jaguars left the factory in 1991 with a colour-coded top panel.

The previous alloy door sill tread plates were replaced from the end of 1985 by a new highly polished stainless steel type, depicting the word 'Jaguar' or 'Daimler' according to marque.

Centre console armrest cubby box comparison shows early Jaguar treatment (top) with a pre-formed plastic finish in black, the Daimler style (centre) with a felt insert that was later adopted for all models, and the much shallower later Series III version (bottom).

Later Series III carpet treatment on the driver's side, with inset rubber heel pad incorporating the marque name. Series III had one-piece underlay with black rubber infills beneath. Note the Velcro fastenings for the top carpets and, in this case, the nylon 'over-rug'.

Bringing the cars up-market during the later years of Series III production, it was decided to fit highly polished stainless steel sill kick plates with a separate inset panel incorporating the marque name.

Headlining & Fittings

Headlining treatment was no different on Series III cars initially, except for the covering on the battens which on this model was black vinyl and not trim-coloured nylon. This black vinyl finish extended down the B/C post trim to the midpoint. From 1981 all Daimlers received the rear quarter reading lamps first seen on the Series II VDP models, although the mounting was different and set into a black vinyl covering. Jaguar Sovereign models also had these lamps as standard from their introduction for 1984. From the 1983 model year all headlinings were standardised with a new colour Limestone finish and a return to matching coverings to the battens and B/C post treatment.

An electric sunroof was now available for all cars. It was operated from a toggle switch, of the same type as used for the window lifts, on the centre console. The underside of the steel sunroof was trimmed in the same nylon material as the headlining, with a felt surround to the headlining edge. The electric sunroof became standard on VDP cars and all V12 Daimlers from August 1982. A black-finished wind deflector, which automatically activated upon opening the roof panel, was supplied with sunroofs from 1986.

With the change to a black vinyl finish for roof battens, the same material was applied to the rear parcel shelf and the central ventilation panel was redesigned with a central press stud. This panel altered again for the 1983 model year with two sculpted cut-outs where it met the rear window.

Sun visors on Series III models were initially finished in black vinyl and recessed into a pre-formed area of the headlining. They were altered in 1985 to match headlining colour.

Series III headlining on a car with an electric sun roof, which gives less headroom for rear seat passengers. Attractive chromed rear reading lamps were first used on the Series I Vanden Plas, then carried forward to all later VDPs, and then to later Series III Jaguar and Daimler models as well.

Initially these had a simple chrome attachment, then a black bracket surround, later changed to trim colour as seen here. Series III sun visors matched trim colour from 1985 and became more elaborate, with a pocket area on the driver's side for paperwork.

Facia & Instruments

This section again must cover the Series models individually, as there were primary changes in the overall design concept of each model range.

Series I

The concept of the XJ Series I facia did not change from 1968 to the end of production in 1973, and its basic format was taken from previous Jaguar saloons from the early '60s.

The facia was surrounded by black foam-based padding. A plastic radio speaker grille was fitted to the centre top of the surround and a swivelling black plastic air vent on each side. The layout followed conventional Jaguar practice, with the two main instruments (rev counter and speedometer) mounted in front of the driver and auxiliary switches and gauges on the centre panel. Initially all the instruments were framed in chrome bezels but a matt black finish was introduced in October

Original Series I dashboard layout, in this case a 4.2-litre version. Note calibration of speedometer and rev counter, and chromed bezels of earlier cars. Radio blanking plate in chrome with black vinyl centre is correct.

Another early Series I dashboard but this time from a 2.8-litre model, with different speedometer and rev counter calibration.

Later Series I dashboard now shows the matt black instrument bezels fitted to all models. This is a Daimler: note steering wheel centre boss badging and matt black surround to heater/radio panel and centre console area.

1970 to prevent glare. Calibration of the rev counter and speedometer varied according to engine size. The 2.8-litre rev counter read to 6000rpm with a red sector from 5500rpm, while the speedometer read to 120mph. The 4.2-litre cars had a 140mph speedometer. On V12s the rev counter went up to 7000rpm with a red sector from 6500rpm, and the speedometer was calibrated to 160mph.

The plastic multi-function warning lamp panel situated between the speedometer and rev counter was the same for all models throughout the production of Series I cars. The black plastic indicator stalk (to the right of the steering column on right-hand drive cars) was the same for all models and all years of Series I production. Within the lower crash-padding area the steering column lock and ignition/starter key switch (to the left of the steering column on right-hand drive cars) was again the same for all models and years of production. Two types of lock were used throughout production, either Waso or Britax, both of the same style and operation.

The smaller Smiths gauges in the centre of the facia were mounted on a black ribbed plastic panel fixed to the wooden facia fillet. These gauges were for (from left) battery condition, oil pressure, analogue clock, water temperature and fuel. Coinciding with the change to black bezels on instruments, the water temperature gauge was changed to provide easier-to-read markings. Similarly in January 1972 a new oil pressure gauge, calibrated to 100psi, was fitted to all cars. Originally gauges had read to 60psi and then to 80psi on interim cars prior to 1972.

A neat row of rocker switches (all of the same style) was sited beneath the gauges in the central facia area. These were to operate exterior and interior lighting, fuel tank changeover, heater fan, wipers, etc. Both the switch-pack and the gauges were fixed on to moulded plastic inserts and then to the centre dash panel.

The whole wooden centre section of the facia hinged down by undoing two black knurled screws, one to either side of the panel, to give access to wiring, instrument bulbs, etc.

Except for some export models, XJs were equipped with an automatic enrichment device instead of a conventional manual choke. Where a manual choke was fitted, operation was by a pull-out black knob with white lettering, fitted to the underside of the facia near the driver's door. An orange choke warning lamp was provided on the driver's side of the facia.

In the centre section above the console was a black flock-covered oddment tray, screwed to the rest of the dash assembly from underneath. Below, on the centre console vertical section, were the controls for heating, ventilation, air conditioning (where fitted) and stereo system. The latter was an extra-cost option on all cars except the Vanden Plas, which initially had an integrated stereo radio and tape player. If stereo equipment was not fitted from new, a chromed blanking panel with padded black Ambla insert was screwed to the console.

Three heating and ventilation sliders were fitted to adjust air flow and direction. These sliders were of the same style, with a black plastic knob traversing a raised chromed slot. On cars without air conditioning a black knurled knob, calibrated in white, was fitted to the right-hand side of the radio panel to adjust temperature. To counter-balance this, on the left-hand side of the radio panel was a similarly shaped blanking plate with the Jaguar name and 'leaper' (scripted 'D' on Daimlers) in silver against a black background. On a car with air conditioning, which was standard only on the VDP, the temperature control was reversed to the left-hand side and the air directional switch, of the same make and style, was situated on the right.

To the far left and right of the facia were the swivelling face level ventilation outlets. The swivelling section was black plastic with a knurled central control knob, while the surround was chromed or black to match instrument bezels.

On the passenger side of the facia was quite a large glovebox with the veneered lid hinged from the base and fitted with a chrome-plated lock which used the same key as the boot lid. Opening the lid cleverly revealed a rectangular vanity mirror angled towards the passenger. The interior of the glovebox was finished in black flock and there was no interior light. The inside of the glovebox lid was always finished in wood veneer.

The steering wheel remained the same on all Series I cars, with the half-moon horn ring always in a matt silver finish. For Jaguars a bronze oval encased the gold 'growler' on the centre boss. On

A V12-engined Series I, in this case a Vanden Plas, with speedometer and rev counter calibrations suitably revised. Gold 'V12' insignia on centre console was fitted to Series I and early Series II V12 cars. Special Vanden Plas features are superior wood veneer figuring, boxwood inlay around the edge of the dashboard, and extra carpeting up the side of the transmission tunnel. V12's manual choke can be seen at lower right, while the separate close-up shows the different choke lever fitted to export six-cylinder cars.

A Series I Daimler with air conditioning (left), and the quality glove compartment finish (below) on all Series I cars.

The forward-facing vertical section of the alloy panel was left etched and blank on cars with manual windows; on cars with electric windows the four chrome-plated slider switches were accommodated in this area.

On Daimler models and Jaguar V12s the same centre console format applied except that the anodised aluminium panel was replaced with a black figured vinyl covering with chromed surround, the same applying to the heating/air conditioning/radio panel. Also on V12 cars, a 'V12' legend in gold was placed on the centre console behind the gear selector quadrant.

Automatic transmission cars had a chromed quadrant lever with black plastic T-bar, which was common to all XJ Series models until the end of production. The quadrant was mounted in a black plastic surround with an illuminated black plastic insert reading 'P R N D 2 1', although this configuration changed in later years with different gearboxes (see *Transmission*, page 100).

Manual transmission cars used a conventional chrome-plated gear lever with black flat-topped knob incorporating the overdrive switch (where fitted) and the gear positions in white lettering. The gear lever gaiter, held in place underneath the alloy console fillet, was in a smooth-finished moulded rubber with three loose folds where it fitted the gear lever.

Series II

With the Series II came an entirely new facia layout with improved safety features, very much in the mould of thinking at the time.

The overall shape of the facia and centre console remained unchanged, with a padded surround and high-quality walnut veneer still used. Revised facia top air vents were used because of complaints that the Series I type deformed with heat after long use, but the radio speaker mounting remained the same.

The first major change came in repositioning all the instruments in front of the driver, so that they were clearly visible through the steering wheel. A revised multi-function warning lamp panel was used, flanked by the smaller speedometer and rev counter but now forming a complete unit. The rev counter and speedometer along with allied lighting remained unchanged until February in the final year of production when, due to changing legislation, it was necessary to calibrate speedometers in both mph and kph in all markets. These revised speedometers also incorporated a warning lamp for the heated rear screen, previously fitted in the rev counter, as well as a bulb-failure warning lamp.

These instruments, along with the four auxiliary gauges, had plastic surrounds with painted

In contrast to the sombre Daimler Series I approach, the bright alloy centre console panel of six-cylinder Series I Jaguars came with complementary chromed sliders. Neat chromed switches on rearward slope are for electric windows – an extra-cost option on Series I models.

Daimlers this had a black background with the scripted 'D' in the centre.

The handbrake on all XJ Series I cars was of the ratchet type, situated against the transmission tunnel alongside the driver's left leg (right-hand drive models); the handle was black. The bonnet release lever, also black finished, was positioned just below the far right-hand side of the facia, within the parcel shelf area.

Etched anodised aluminium inset trim covered the upholstered area around the gearbox and led back to the console armrest/glovebox. Secured by self-tapping chromed Phillips screws, the alloy panel was cut out to accept the two chrome-plated ashtrays common to all Series I and II cars.

Behind the right-hand ashtray was the cigar lighter, this position being common to all Series saloons. On the Series I and II models the lighter unit had a simple circular black knob without any legend. To the left of this in the adjacent position was a circular 'marker' within the panel to indicate where additional switches could be sited. This was usually reserved for a balance control when multi-speaker radio equipment was fitted.

Series II dashboard layout on six-cylinder Jaguar models. Calibration of speedometer and rev counter still altered according to engine size.

Much revised centre console treatment on the Series II models, with new switchgear, clock, raised parcel shelf and heater/air conditioning panel. Period 8-track stereo on this Jaguar (left) was part of the extra-cost option packages available when new. Black centre console treatment (above) was used on all V12-engined cars and six-cylinder Daimlers. Side view shows the new switchgear style for electric windows, plus the fifth toggle switch to isolate the rear windows from use by children (this fifth switch was between the two lower rocker switches on early Series II models). The other rocker switch, on the lower console section, activated central door locking. This particular car, a 1977 V12 Coupé, does not feature the gold 'V12' insignia on the console.

Cheapened glove compartment interior on Series II and all subsequent Series III models, with plastic instead of veneered backing panel to the lid, and revised mirror.

silver finishes. These minor gauges were oil pressure (top left of rev counter), battery condition (bottom left of rev counter), fuel (top right of speedometer) and water temperature (bottom right of speedometer).

Face-level ventilators set into the extreme ends of the facia were in the same positions as on Series I cars, but were now rectangular and again matched the instruments with a silver-painted surround. They also featured 'sticker' legends on a silver background to indicate direction of flow. This silver finish continued in the form of a plastic strip that followed the contour of the wooden facia around the edges at the base. The silver finish to instruments, air vents, etc, was dropped in July 1978 for the remaining cars produced.

The centre section of the facia was now an integral part of the wooden facia and veneering. To replace the auxiliary gauges on the Series I cars, a new full-width plastic air vent assembly with three sections was fitted to match the face vents at either side. The outer sections were adjustable for direction and flow while the inner section

provided air to the rest of the car. Underneath this was the oddments shelf, now in a much higher position to leave room for the auxiliary switch panel and new rectangular clock (again finished with painted silver border). The four push-button switches were for (from left) fuel tank changeover switch, heated rear window, map lamp and interior lamp. These switches and the clock were inset into a pre-moulded plastic panel finished in black with silver facing.

On the passenger side the glovebox received a new style lock surround with integrated black plastic 'pull'. The interior of the glovebox lid was now fitted with a black plastic face providing a flat area to hold drinks, etc, to the left and the vanity mirror to the right under a spring-loaded white clip. The interior was still flock-finished and illuminated on Vanden Plas models only.

Black pre-formed fibre panels were screwed to the underside of the facia to hide electrics, etc. Black plastic levers controlled the bonnet release and manual choke (where fitted to V12s) as with

Early Series III centre console had new treatment, with black fabric covering and recessed style of cigar lighter on all cars.

the Series I cars, and the handbrake was of the same style in the same position. Also to the far left and far right undersides of the facia were two controls to regulate air to the footwells, as on the later Series I cars, by means of push/pull black knobs with white legends.

The remaining layout of the centre console was like the Series I cars except for a change in control knob and legend style (now on the alloy fillet) for heating and air conditioning systems

Post-1982 Series III dashboard and centre console arrangement. Note the new style instrumentation on Series IIIs and the new steering wheel. Brass plaque on centre console signifies that this is the last six-cylinder car produced.

Late model, top-of-the-range Jaguar Sovereign has new style centre console treatment, with computer and extra veneering to the lower section, plus final CD stereo equipment and two-stage air conditioning controls adapted from XJ40 system. Side view shows additional toggle switch on the 'upbank' for the electric sunroof.

Until the introduction of Jaguar Sovereign models a computer was not fitted either as standard or an extra-cost option. In such cases, after the introduction of the revised Series III centre console layout, an analogue clock of the type used on Series II cars was fitted. This could also be specified on any car right to the end of production if a computer was not required.

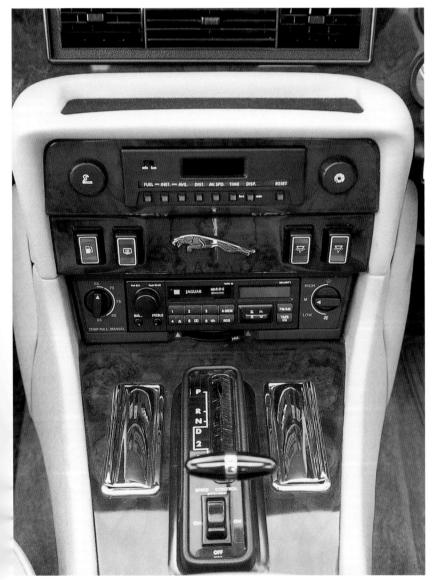

and new-style substantial black rocker switches to control electric windows. The same style of rocker switch was also used for the auxiliary switch area below the left-hand ashtray. On Series II cars this was used to activate the central-locking system, which at this time was not controlled by the door locks. A fifth slighter smaller rocker switch, which isolated the rear electric windows (for child safety), was also fitted to the vertical section of the centre console.

As with the Series I models, both V12s and Daimlers had the centre console finished in black figured vinyl, although the radio, heater and air conditioning panel remained in a bright alloy finish until July 1978, when all cars were fitted with the matt fabric covering. As radios were still an extra-cost option on most models, the same style of black blanking plate was used in the radio area on the console.

With the adoption of totally new heating and air conditioning systems came the feature of footwell ventilators in the form of plastic rectangular units secured by two chromed screws to the upholstered 'cheeks' of the centre console area.

With the advent of modernisation and ergonomics, Jaguar followed the trend with the addition of windscreen wash/wipe controls to a stalk on the left-hand side of the steering column, matching the indicator stalk on the right. Both stalks were plastic with satin-finish plastic inserts containing black legends. Similar treatment was given to the external lighting switch, now a circular knob fitted in the ignition position of Series I cars. The ignition switch, again with a similar satin-finish panel, was now in the adjacent position to the right of the steering column.

For the first time on any British car, Jaguar adopted fibre-optic lighting cables for some of the controls. For more on this aspect see the *Electrics* chapter (page 72).

The steering wheel was of an entirely new design, 1in smaller in diameter than on the Series I. It contained the same style of Jaguar 'growler' in gold on a brown background or, in the case of Daimlers, a gold 'D' with a black background. No horn ring was fitted to Series II steering wheels, so the horns were now operated by pushing any part of the centre oval boss.

Coupé models and Daimlers were equipped in exactly the same way as the normal saloons.

Series III

Although the interior was redesigned from the Series II, the facia wood remained unchanged – but some minor changes took place with instrumentation, controls and the centre console.

The most striking change was in the steering wheel. Another new design with a stepped centre boss allowed better visibility between the horizontal spokes. The same wheel was used on all models of Jaguar and Daimler, except that centre boss badging altered to suit. In November 1982 Daimler models received a new thicker-rimmed wheel with the Daimler name in chrome and inset within the rubberised fabric boss, which itself had been restyled with ribbed ends. No other steering wheel changes took place except when the factory began to run out of stock for the very last Jaguar V12s. In these cases the later XJ-S sports-style wheel with recessed horn pushes was used, sometimes accompanied by the later, smoother indicator and wiper stalks on the steering column. These changes applied from the 1991 model year.

Speedometer, rev counter and auxiliary gauges were all supplied by Smiths and, although of the same size as on the last Series IIs, were of very different design. Both the larger instruments had heavy black cowled surrounds and incorporated new legends and square warning lamps. The minor gauges, although following the same general style and calibration as Series II models, had symbols instead of words, thus eliminating the need for Jaguar to change instruments according to market. Similarly the central multi-function warning lamp unit was of a totally different style and operation from the Series II version.

Most of the above elements remained the same throughout Series III production, although minor changes took place to warning lamp operation, and speedometer and rev counter calibration altered according to engine size as before. However, in April 1982 Jaguar opted to change all the auxiliary instruments from Smiths to Veglia, although the general style was the same. Vanden

Very last V12-engined Jaguar Sovereign models received this new style (XJ-S) steering wheel of smaller dimensions and incorporating horn push buttons at either side.

Plas gauges did not change until about six months later, presumably to use up stocks.

During the last years of Series III production, from the 1991 model year, Jaguar and Daimler V12s were fitted with ABS (anti-lock braking), bringing an accompanying rectangular warning lamp to the facia on the driver's side.

On the centre console the only change came with the cigar lighter, which was now recessed into the panel with a revised knob and legend. Lastly the lids of the twin chromed ashtrays were now shaped with smoother edged lips to avoid cutting fingers when opening. From mid-1981 the heating/air conditioning/radio alloy panel was replaced by a matt black item.

As early Series III models were available with a manual five-speed gearbox, the gear lever was now in black with a new-style knob with curved top incorporating the white gear position legend. A more substantial leather gaiter was used on Series III cars. Where automatic transmission was fitted the same style was employed from Series I and II models, although the base was lengthened to accommodate the rocker switch for cruise control operation (where fitted).

A much larger rear-view mirror was fitted to

a chromed Jaguar 'leaper' or 'Daimler' script appeared. For the first time this stepped panel was made from aluminium with walnut veneer applied by a heat process. The area underneath the conventional heating/air conditioning control panel (now black with new switchgear and legends) and radio position was unchanged.

The centre console around the gear lever (or quadrant) was of the same style but now simplified, without the need to accommodate a cigar lighter, etc. Because of the stepped nature of the upper console area, the automatic transmission quadrant was moved back fractionally on the console to allow sufficient clearance when the lever was in the 'Park' position.

With the adoption of a Mark III air conditioning system (similar to that used on the later XJ40 models) in July 1986, new switchgear was needed again on the console. This area was further amended for the 1991 model year when the new-style Clarion radio/tape/CD player was fitted. To accommodate the new audio system, the position of the air conditioning panel and controls was slightly revised and hoses were routed below the new brake pipes that ran across the bulkhead.

In mid-1985 changes were made to veneering with the adoption of a fully-veneered centre console panel around the automatic transmission quadrant. With this change came the use of straight-grain veneer across this console and the whole facia area on all 3.4-litre models.

Where cars were equipped with an electric sunroof, the black rocker switch (of the same type as used for electric window lifts) was accommodated in the centre of the vertical console area, with the window switches.

In 1983 Jaguar offered an on-board trip computer in a rectangular (radio style) format with crackle black finish. It became standard on Jaguar Sovereign and Daimler V12 models, and the same unit was offered for all models of XJ and also to subsequent XJ-S models. Where fitted, the unit took the place of the analogue clock, as the trip computer incorporated a digital clock anyway. The computer was upgraded for the 1984 model year, providing the facility to run the mileage trip to 999.9 miles (instead of 99.9). Internally the new computer contained CMOS technology to prevent power surge damage to memory information. Quite simple to operate, the computer provided information on the amount of fuel left, fuel consumption at any given moment (updated every 15 seconds), distance travelled on a journey and since filling up with fuel, average speed, time, and time elapsed on journeys since reset.

As with the majority of models, sound equipment remained an extra-cost option for the Series III. This aspect is covered in the *Optional Equipment & Accessories* chapter (page 114).

Last of the production Daimler Double Sixes, with revised steering wheel centre. Note the adoption of a Daimler script on the centre console to replace the Jaguar 'leaper' and the additional rectangular warning light below the speedometer for the ABS system fitted on very late models.

Series III models. Indicator and wiper stalks on the column were changed in position to match common European standards.

The facia-mounted glovebox arrangement was exactly as on the Series II cars but from 1981 interior illumination became a standard feature on all models.

For the 1983 model year the facia was changed in detail, along with a new centre section and console. Out came all the brightwork that had been carried over from the Series II, such as the surround to the base of the facia, the steering column stalks and light switch/ignition switch, the latter now black with new legends.

A new centre section console was fitted leading down from the facia. The shallower pre-formed oddments tray was now positioned much higher, nearer the air conditioning vents, under which was fitted the analogue clock. It was flanked by a large black rheostat facia lighting switch (with white legend) to the right and new-style matching cigar lighter re-sited to the left. The panel then stepped inwards to where the traditional rectangular auxiliary switches were now positioned in the same layout and format as before. In the position normally left for the clock,

Electrics

All Series XJs used a conventional 12-volt negative earth electrical system. An integrated wiring harness ran from a single battery normally mounted in the engine bay. Only the very last V12 Series III models had the battery in the boot.

Wiring

A single wiring harness ran the length and width of the car from the under-bonnet area. It was strapped to the inner wings and then ran down through the inner dashboard area, along the top of each sill and then from Series II models along the transmission tunnel to the base of the rear seat pan and into the boot.

The wiring loom was encased in PVC and the general principle remained the same throughout the life of the models. Different harnesses were used for the long-wheelbase models and then for the VDP cars. Harnesses changed completely an amazing number of times for all models in accord with production changes throughout the life of the cars. The final change came in 1990 with the introduction of catalytic converters, which required take-offs for the two Lambda sensors on the cylinder banks. The addition of fuel injection simply meant an extra loom especially for this.

From the Series II, models with the 'sealed bulkhead' wiring harness connection into and out of the bulkhead terminated in multi-pin male and female plugs finished in yellow, white or black according to function.

Battery

The original Series I had a 12-volt battery situated in the nearside bulkhead area under the bonnet (right-hand drive cars). This was a large battery by later Series II and III standards. Terminals were of the push-on type with braided leads and rubberised covers provided for each terminal, red or black to signify polarity. The battery was encased in a black metal surround clamped to the base of the bulkhead by two threaded rods; location was by separately bolted-on hooks at the base of the battery tray. The battery itself was also mounted on to a separate tray.

The simple battery carrier of earlier Series I six-cylinder cars, both 2.8 and 4.2, showing the attached screen wash reservoir.

A revised type of battery carrier, incorporating a battery cooling fan, was found on V12 and later six-cylinder Series Is, and most Series II cars as well.

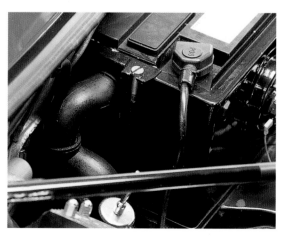

To prevent build-up of gases, cars equipped with the battery cooling fan had a special battery box vent feeding into the scuttle plenum drain.

For the last V12 cars equipped with ABS, the battery and connections were moved to the boot, freeing engine bay space for the ABS actuator equipment and relevant pipework.

The same basic layout applied to all subsequent models until 1991 when, because of the fitting of ABS, the battery was moved to the boot bulkhead. There it was positioned on the left-hand side with its own black metal retaining tray welded to the base of the boot supports. The battery was protected by a grained black plastic cover held in position by two finger-grip screws.

Returning to the under-bonnet battery position, a change occurred in the fitting surround in 1972 with the introduction of the V12 engine. Because of the immense heat generated by the V12 installation, it was felt necessary to fit a small battery cooling fan within the black steel casing. The fan was activated automatically by a sensor when the temperature around the battery exceeded 55°C.

This battery cooling fan was standardised on all models and continued unchanged on Series III cars until December 1981, when the fan was deleted from all six-cylinder models, and then V12 cars from the end of Series II production.

Ancillaries

Various aspects of the electrical equipment are discussed elsewhere in the *Body Trim* (page 26) and *Interior Trim* (page 44) chapters, and the position of components such as coils and relays can be

identified easily from under-bonnet photographs in the *Engine* chapter (page 77).

The alternator was initially a Lucas 11 AC, later 11 ACR, with 20 ACR for air conditioned cars. The mounting bracket and adjusters were finished in black with the alternator itself left as natural metal along with the relevant pulleys. On an air conditioned car the alternator position was lower, to accommodate the compressor.

Horns were situated on the front suspension cross-member, bolted directly to it or, in the case of air conditioned cars, on a stepped pillar to clear the alternator position. On late Series II and subsequent cars the horn was moved to an under-bumper position. Two horns, with different tones and finished in black, were fitted in all cases.

The pre-engaged starter motor on all cars was of Lucas type M45G, always finished in black with a black heavy-duty electrical feed connection.

The ignition coil was of the ballast type and a conventional Lucas type 22D distributor with black plastic cap was fitted. From August 1970 a modified distributor with top-entry cap and push-in connectors was adopted. This also coincided with the arrival of HT leads with radio/television suppression conductors. From February 1974 all V12 engines, from engine number 7P.8169, received a new 'high load' coil and amplifier to improve sparking plug performance.

Series I six-cylinder coils were mounted on the right-hand inner wing, adjacent to the ballast resistor. Series II coils and ballast resistors were mounted on the engine. Series III 4.2 and any Series II fuel injection six-cylinder engines had the coil mounted on top of the inlet manifold, but on the 3.4-litre the coil remained on the engine.

When the V12 engine became available in the XJ saloon Lucas produced a special ignition system called OPUS (Oscillating Pick-Up System). This used solid-state circuitry, which was advanced for the time. In March 1979 all V12s received a new Lucas AB3 electronic ignition amplifier for better reliability. This was also much smaller and, for ease of accessibility, was fitted to the radiator cross-member from VIN 111703. Earlier models could be retro-fitted in this way.

With the V12 also came the first use of an electric engine cooling fan. Made by Airscrew using a Bosch motor, this had four blades and a black finish. For the last few months of Series II production, strategic markets in hot countries such as Japan, Australia and the US had cars fitted with twin electric fans.

To improve ignition performance, 4.2-litre engines from the 1985 model year (from engine 8L.173271) received a new Ducellier coil, ballast resistor, modified amplifier (black instead of silver) and harness bolted to the flat end of the inlet manifold. On very late V12 engines (from

7P.62208 SA) a single Marelli solid-state ignition coil, distributor and king lead assembly was fitted. New style Lucar terminals meant that this was not interchangeable with earlier models and that the forward-mounted auxiliary coil and associated harness were deleted.

Fuse boxes varied dramatically throughout the production life of the cars, starting with the Series I where twin fuse boxes were fitted behind the traditional fold-down centre dash panel. Each box held five fuses. In addition Series I XJs used in-line fuses throughout the car. Series II models also made use of in-line fuses, but there were also two small auxiliary fuse boxes fitted to each side of the radiator top rail; these controlled the main and dip headlamp functions. The Series II main fuse for the horn feed was situated in line above and behind the brake servo.

The Series II style of fuse box carried on to Series III with the main fuse box contained underneath the driver's side dash liner, accessed via a removable hatch. This was bolted on to the blower motor housings. In all cases fuses were of the circular glass tube type.

Series III models also had an auxiliary fuse box on the passenger side dash liner, again with the same types of glass fuses. Series III XJs also introduced a much more comprehensive fuse box on the nearside front inner wing to control the electric cooling fan and the dip and main headlamp beams. Earlier cars with an electric cooling fan had an in-line fuse just above the cooling fan itself; this applied to Series I V12s as well. In-line fuses were also placed in the driver's side centre console on Series IIIs (to control cigar lighter, etc), in the boot (to control aerial circuitry), behind the radio (to control its functions) and on the boot fire wall (to control the sunroof, where fitted). The very last Series IIIs went to blade-type fuses in new boxes.

Wiper motors were from Lucas, predominantly of the same type. From the introduction of Series III models the shutdown operation was amended, with one-stop parking instead of the 'dancing' arrangement to correct the lie of the blades when switching off. At the same time an intermittent 6sec wipe facility was added via a delay relay, coloured blue and fitted underneath the passenger side dashboard liner.

Interior lighting was conventional except that with the introduction of the Series II models there was an integrated fibre-optic lighting arrangement. A single bulb located in a special housing underneath the centre console (just behind the gear selector quadrant) provided illumination for a number of fibre-optic cables which then went to the heater/fan and ignition/headlamp controls. As Series II progressed to Series III, with more buttons added to the heating and ventilation con-

The earliest fitting of the horn (left), on the front subframe behind the alternator, applied to cars without air conditioning. Cars with air conditioning, both Series I and II, had the horn raised and brought back towards the centre of the engine mount (below left). On late Series II models onwards the horns were re-positioned yet again to an under-bumper location.

trols, so the number of fibre-optic cables increased accordingly.

From August 1979 (at VIN 302107) a new rheostat switch with a minimum brightness stop was incorporated for instrument lighting.

On the aesthetic side, the rear screen was altered in December 1970 and became a 'hot line' heated type identifiable by the horizontal heater element wiring switchable from the dashboard. From the introduction of the Series III models, the rear screen heating elements were controlled by a timer that switched them off after 15 minutes.

Central locking was made available on Series

Changes to relays, wiring , fuse boxes, etc, were numerous on Series I/II/III models. Two typical examples are fuel injection relays situated against the bulkhead (right) and other relays on a late Series III radiator top rail (below).

(LHD) and 429455 (RHD), to incorporate full electric motor operation for doors and boot instead of the previous electro-solenoid system.

For the 1983 model year onwards an on-board computer became available. Sited in the upper centre console panel, it necessitated another new wiring harness to incorporate an inter-face unit between the fuel injection ECU and the speedometer and trip computer.

A sunroof, always electrically operated, was only available from the factory on Series III models. The motor and fuses were situated in the boot at the side of the rear bulkhead.

At the end of 1985 a diode was fitted within the circuitry of the radio aerial to safeguard against a sticking aerial blowing a fuse. Jaguar Service requested dealers to retro-fit this to all earlier cars.

To comply with legislative requirements, from November 1986 all UK-specification cars received a dipped headlight circuit to be illuminated in a dimmed condition when the side lights were switched on. This modification applied from VIN 469301.

In 1990 German-market models were fitted with a headlamp levelling system from VIN 482508. This affected only the outer headlamps, which were adjusted by a small electric motor situated beneath the lamp assembly. Operation was from the switch normally used for the map-reading light, the wiring of which was redirected to the interior light switch, which then served both functions.

At the same time Canadian legislation dictated that dipped-beam headlamps, plus side and number plate lamps, should be illuminated at all times when the engine was running. This involved fitting three relays on a bracket to the bulkhead wall adjacent to the brake booster.

From February 1990 cigar lighter electrics were amended so that the lighters would only work with the ignition switch in positions '1' or '2', and not when switched off.

Heating & Air Conditioning

With the new XJ6, many people commented that the company had provided a 'decent' heating and ventilation system for the first time on any Jaguar. It was significantly more efficient than on earlier models, but also more complex and sophisticated. Smiths designed and built the system for Jaguar.

Air was drawn in through the grille on top of the scuttle area to a chamber where the air, heated or ambient, could be distributed. A complicated but nevertheless efficient system of flap valves was employed to direct that air to the interior of the car to suit the occupants. Generating the equivalent of 5¼kW of heating, the system was capable of heating 160cu ft of air per minute to 82°C and

II models (except 3.4-litre cars) and was actuated from within the cockpit by a switch located on the centre console. This meant that the driver's door still had to be locked and unlocked manually, and entrance through this door did not automatically open the other doors. With the Series III came an entirely new system, which included electro-locking of the boot with one key operation. From VIN 346688 (around November 1982) the system was altered so operation of the passenger door exterior lock no longer locked the whole car.

Central-locking systems were further amended in September 1985, from VINs 428715

distributing it to any of five points. There were two outlets on the dashboard top panel (one each side), two ducts in the footwells and a further outlet at the rear of the centre console (not used on the 2.8-litre 'Standard' model).

Two electric fans provided forced movement of the air via a two-position switch on the facia. These black-finished fans were mounted within the engine bay and operated through holes in the bulkhead. Air conditioned 4.2s and all V12s had aluminium heat shielding glued to the engine face of the bulkhead.

Temperature selection came from a heat-sensing tap with a setting control on the centre console calibrated in numbers. Opening and closing of relevant flaps of air direction also came from levers and control cables via the console. Cool ambient air was fed from the plenum chamber to the face-level ventilators in the facia and rear compartment. Stale air was cleverly extracted from the interior through a one-way outlet in the centre of the rear parcel shelf, leading to a low-pressure area below the rear window in a gap between the boot lid and rear bodywork.

An optional air conditioning system, made by Delaney Gallay, was also offered on all Series I models. The evaporator unit was designed to fit into the existing heating system without taking up valuable space elsewhere in the interior or boot. Unlike later Jaguars, and much more akin to modern air conditioning, the system on the Series I XJ could be switched on and off separately from the heater. Additional relays were provided to ensure that the blower motors came on automatically if the air conditioning was switched on. Otherwise lack of air flow through the evaporator could cause damage.

A calibrated knob on the centre console (replacing the marque name badge) altered the temperature of the air conditioning system. The opposite knob control (for heater temperature on cars without air conditioning) changed to an air directional control.

For the Series II models an entirely new system, called Delanair, was developed to provide a more efficient heating system and completely automatic air conditioning. In essence this was effectively a true climate-control system. It was optional on all models, but became a more frequent sight, particularly on V12s.

For air conditioned cars the temperature rotary control was moved to the left of the console and controlled in a span of 20°F (marked 65, 70, 75, 80, 85). The 'Air Flow' knob on the right-hand side of the console again controlled fan speed but with a central 'Auto' position, which used sensors to control the fan speed automatically to achieve the temperature required.

The system operated in a similar manner to the

Series I models, with air entering the car from the base of the windscreen vent. Air then passed through the evaporator matrix, where it was cooled and dehumidified, then on to the four blending flaps. Plastic parts of the system were black and metal was either left natural or finished in black. Sensing thermistors automatically operated a servo motor to work the series of flaps. Flaps were black and the rods connecting the servo to the flaps from the servo were bright metal.

For the 1985 model year all 4.2-litre cars were fitted with a revised receiver/dryer which was moved to ensure the maximum refrigerant flow. The sight glass was moved to the left in a vertical position; V12s remained unaltered at this time.

The same system continued unchanged into Series III production except for minor changes to the operational controls on the centre console and the hot/cold air slide to the face vents.

In July 1986, however, came a revised air conditioning system (known as the Mark III) with a computer-controlled module pre-dating the same system later used on XJ40 models. Apart from additional wiring, the visible changes were that the old electro-vacuum servo system was replaced by a pair of flap servo motors and the four flaps became two. An entirely new low-gas protection clutch system for the compressor, incorporating a thermal fuse, was also fitted at this time. This thermal fuse and the super-heat switch in the air conditioning system were deleted in December 1991 and replaced by an HSLP (High Side Low Pressure) switch from VIN 471852.

Inside the car, the temperature selector switch now had a ratchet feel and also had a push/pull auto/manual mode. Temperature slides at the base also now controlled flap motors electrically instead of by cable. Controls on the centre console were altered to a new, squarer style with matt black finish and new legends.

An early Series I XJ6 showing the conventional heater blower motor position within the engine bay. Also visible is an intact long plenum drain pipe, which has usually disappeared or been shortened on cars today.

Engine

There was nothing new about any of the engines used in the Series I, II or III Jaguar and Daimler models. So much has been written before that it is only necessary here to recap on the overall design, applications and differences in specification, fitting and finish according to model.

The XK six-cylinder power unit, introduced in 1948, had powered every subsequent Jaguar up to the introduction of the XJ6 in 1968. The 5.3-litre V12 engine had been introduced in 1971, prior to the XJ12, for the Series III E-type, but actually was always intended for the saloon.

Twin overhead camshafts, six cylinders in line, a straight-port aluminium cylinder head and a cast iron block was the basic specification of the XK engine. The camshafts were driven by separate top and bottom Reynolds duplex timing chains and actuated two valves per cylinder in hemispherical

combustion chambers, the latter designed by Harry Weslake. Alloy pistons featured chrome-plated top rings with wide-blade steel connecting rods. Lubrication was by a pump gear-driven from the front of the crankshaft.

All the XK power units fitted to XJ saloons were of the same basic exterior design. All used ribbed cam covers in black with appropriate Jaguar or Daimler logos on the inlet cam cover. On Series I and some Series II models the oil filler cap, situated on the exhaust cam cover, was a conventional polished alloy cap as used on earlier cars. From N-registered models the cap changed to a black-finished metal design with two ears for ease of removal. Cylinder heads were all painted silver, as were the engine lifting brackets fitted to the exterior of the heads. Engine blocks were all painted black. The sump remained unpainted on

The 2.8-litre Series I XJ6. Note the differences between this and the larger-engined cars. The engine is set lower into the frame and the radiator expansion tank is on top of the radiator itself, with appropriately re-routed pipework. Black plastic finishers on the sharp edges of the outer wings, where they meet the inner wings, often extended the full length of the join, but not always. The drilled cam cover is not original.

all models. The individual engine bay photographs show specific areas of finish and layout applicable to the various models unless otherwise identified in the captions.

Some design changes concerned all engines, such as when a new oil sump strainer was fitted to overcome cavitation. This took place from engine numbers 7G.8383 (2.8) and 7L.12104 (4.2), but in many cases it was fitted retrospectively to earlier engines. In October 1969 the engine rear mounting centre bracket assembly was changed to a harder compound, to eliminate vibration. From mid-1970 the design of the sump was changed from the initial finned type to a flat-based type subsequently used on all models. In December 1970 Jaguar engine numbers changed to show letters (replacing figures) to indicate compression ratios: 'H' for High compression (9.0: 1), 'S' for Standard (8.0: 1) and 'L' for Low (7.0:1).

Series I

2.8-litre

Although the XK engine was well known to everyone, the 2.8-litre version was an entirely new configuration specifically designed for the XJ6. Throughout development a 3-litre version had

been planned but never came to fruition. To cater for certain export markets where taxes were based on engine capacity, Jaguar decided on the 2.8-litre version as a secondary alternative to the existing 4.2-litre power unit used in most Series I cars.

The 2.8-litre engine was fitted to Series I cars and to a few early Series II models. Its precise capacity was 2792cc, from a bore and stroke of 83×86mm, and it developed 180bhp (gross) at 6000rpm. Standard compression ratio was 9.0:1, but 8.0:1 was optional.

The 2.8-litre XJ engine was only ever fitted to the XJ Series saloons so there is no crossover with other Jaguar models. The basic layout of the unit in situ is no different from any other XK-engined Series XJ saloon, but a major difference is that the 2.8-litre sits lower in the engine bay because of its shorter stroke.

The main problem with the 2.8-litre unit was its propensity to hole pistons. This problem was never identified during development and testing because the engines were always run at near maximum revs, preventing the build-up of carbon on the piston crowns that subsequently came about during conventional road use.

As for changes to the 2.8-litre engine, there were very few during the brief period of produc-

The 4.2-litre Series I XJ6, inlet side. This early car shows the original style of radiator expansion tank on the far inner wing. On post-1970 cars this changed to the same style used on the Series II models (see pages 82-83). The position of the screen washer reservoir bottle also changed to match the Series II cars at this point. This engine correctly shows non-drilled cam covers.

The 4.2-litre Series I XJ6, exhaust side. Manifolding was always supplied vitreous enamelled on the Series I, although this finish tends to deteriorate quickly. The bright, convoluted engine breather pipe at the front of the engine exits to atmosphere, whereas later models had a recycling system into the engine block. Note the correct fitting and colour of engine lifting brackets.

tion. The flared metal intake on the air cleaner produced depressions in the air cleaner itself, so a new air cleaner (part C.31073/1), which featured a neoprene flared intake, was fitted from October 1969. At the same time a modified inlet manifold (part C.31975) was also fitted, shortened at the front to provide better access to the distributor for contact breaker point adjustment. In November 1969, from engine number 7G.5795, the quest for quieter running brought revised camshafts, recognisable by the addition of a groove machined in the periphery of the end flange.

January 1970 saw the introduction of new cylinder head cam covers incorporating drilled and tapped mounting holes for the exhaust emissions air ducts, from engine number 7G6125. In March 1970 Jaguar recommended the exhaust valve clearances were amended from 0.006in to 0.008in and a month later specified the use of Champion N7Y sparking plugs instead of N9Y. Uprated pistons were fitted from engine number 7G.8849 and, in fact, installed in earlier engines when owners complained after breakdowns.

From April 1971 an improved crankshaft rear oil seal was also fitted to all 2.8-litre engines. From December 1971, at engine number 7G.16343, an oil pump with a die-cast body was used.

4.2-litre

The mainstay of XJ Series production was the 4.2-litre version of the XK engine, as originally seen in the Jaguar 420 and Daimler Sovereign models from the late '60s. This engine went on to feature in all Series XJ models in different guises. All the 4.2-litre XJ engines had a capacity of 4235cc and initially developed 245bhp (gross) at 5500rpm and 283lb ft of torque at 3750rpm. The standard compression ratio was 8.0:1, although engines with 7.0:1 or 9.0:1 compression were available to special order.

The XK engine was adapted for use in the XJ6 by the use of a larger impeller to the water pump to aid engine cooling and a bigger diameter by-pass hose. On the cylinder head, the water holes were made larger on the exhaust side and correspondingly in the block to provide for more even running temperature. Longer studs were used in the block and a new style of viscous-coupling engine fan was installed. No other changes were made to this engine as previously fitted to the Jaguar 420 model.

Development changes on the 4.2-litre engine during Series I production included new camshafts, as on the 2.8-litre, from November 1969 (at engine number 7L.8344), to provide

Typical early V12 installation with the four Stromberg 175 CD carburettors and without air conditioning. Air cleaners are correctly painted black, although some very early examples (including cars used for brochure photography) featured 'crackle' silver like the Series I six-cylinder models. Note also the finned ignition amplifier situated within the engine vee, the correct lie of all pipework, and the correct style of 'discs' (four in total) to separate the HT leads.

The 3.4-litre Series II engine bay. As on all Series II models and late Series I cars, an exhaust emissions system is fitted to this car and also incorporates engine breather trunking to the carburettors and the AED. The screen wash electric pump is incorrectly positioned on the far inner wing, a common change carried out by garages because of the difficulty of accessing the pump in its normal position, underneath the bulkhead just to the left of centre.

quieter valve operation, and the use of emission-type exhaust manifolds in March 1970. In the same month the camshaft sprocket adjuster plate, with vernier adjustment, was replaced by a new type with lobes. However, after a recall most of these were replaced to the previous specification. From March 1970 the new cam covers with drilled holes to take emissions air ducts were fitted to 4.2s (from engine 7L.8474), as on 2.8-litre cars.

June 1970 saw the introduction of a small black guard over the fan at the front of the alternator for safety reasons. From December 1971 the 4.2-litre followed the 2.8 with the use of a die-cast oil pump body from engine number 7L.31456.

5.3-litre

From the start the Jaguar V12 engine had been developed for the XJ saloon but initially was fitted into the Series III E-type in 1971 and was only introduced into the XJ bodyshell from 11 July 1972. The design concept was very similar to the XK power unit, the V12 also having chain-driven overhead camshafts and an alloy cylinder head.

The 5343cc engine had a bore and stroke of 90.0×70.0mm. It produced 253bhp at 6000rpm and 302lb ft of torque at 3500rpm with a compression ratio of 9.0:1. Engine block and cylinder

heads were made entirely from aluminium. With one cylinder head per bank of six cylinders, the engine was fuelled through no fewer than four Zenith-Stromberg 175CD SE carburettors placed outside the vee. The crankshaft, of EN16T steel, had seven main bearings, an oil cooler was fitted and a 17in diameter steel engine cooling fan with viscous coupling was used.

From July 1972, a neoprene collar insert was fitted to V12 engines over the oil dipstick to prevent oil surge in extreme circumstances. This altered the oil capacity of the engine to 19 pints, and a new type of dipstick was subsequently fitted. Specific engine bay changes over the period included the move of the chassis plate from the left wing valance to the right in June 1972.

Series II

2.8-litre

Only 170 of the 2.8-litre cars were turned out with Series II bodyshells and the installation was the same as on the later Series I versions.

3.4-litre

New with the introduction of the Series II model, to replace the 2.8-litre version, came another XK

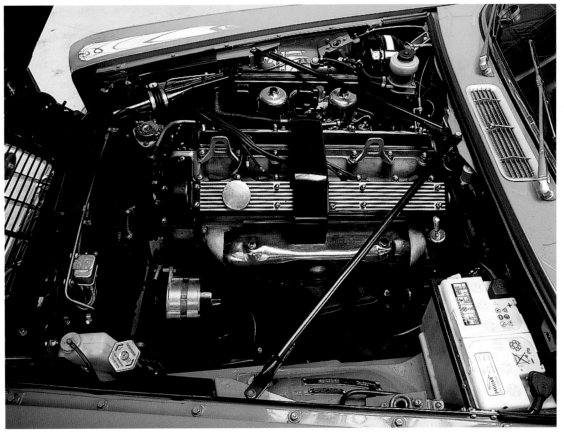

The Series II 4.2-litre engine installation, without air conditioning. The two-piece black plastic covering on the outer-to-inner wing join extends the full length of the wings. Exhaust side shows the bright heat shielding to the manifolds, which were no longer vitreous enamelled. The radiator expansion tank pressure cap is incorrect.

A later 4.2-litre Series II equipped with air conditioning. Note the fuel cooler across the back of the carburettor area (these are the later carburettors) and the correct lie of air conditioning piping and fittings. Exhaust side shows the later full-width heat shields to the manifolds and the position of the air conditioning compressor, which has displaced the alternator to a lower level. 'P' clips on the engine bay cross-braces support the pipes to stop chafing. Midway through Series II production the oil filler cap changed from the conventional alloy type with a milled edge to an easier-to-use black alloy design with eared grips.

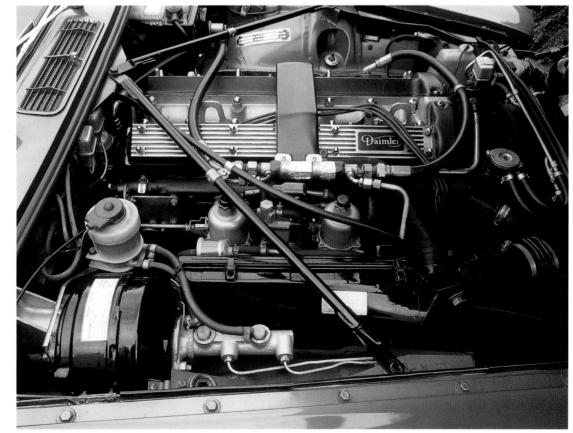

engine configuration, this time bringing back a size made famous at the beginning of engine production in 1948 with the XK120. The 3.4-litre unit was never fitted to Coupé models and was never made available in the US market.

Of the same 3442cc as the old engine, the new unit had a bore and stroke of 83.0×106.0mm. The block, however, was entirely different, having enlarged cooling passages and external ribbing to increase rigidity and strength. Grooved main bearings were used to increase oil flow. Following normal XJ practice, carburation was by twin SUs, with an automatic choke system as on the 4.2-litre unit. Power output was 161bhp (DIN) at 5000rpm and maximum torque was 189lb ft at 3500rpm.

From engine number 8A.7841 improved Tuftrided exhaust valves were fitted to all subsequent units. A disposable oil filter canister was fitted from engine number 8A.101372.

4.2-litre

A new air cleaner assembly was fitted to all Series II XJ6 engines, which had a new thermostatically-controlled, exhaust-heated, air intake system to reduce emissions. The compression ratio was also changed from 8.0:1 to 7.8:1. These changes had the effect of strangling the engine output, which dropped to 170bhp (DIN) at 4500rpm. At the same time a Clayton Dewandre single-tube oil cooler was fitted, mainly to cars for Police work but some civilian models also had it.

In March 1978 4.2-litre engines were fitted with a disposable oil filter assembly from engine number 8L.70840. There were two types of filter head, one allowing horizontal fitment, the other vertical. From engine number 8L.51581 improved Tuftrided exhaust valves were fitted as on 3.4-litre engines.

May 1978 saw the first of the fuel-injected 4.2-litre engines. The Lucas-Bosch L-Jetronic system increased output to 176bhp and was supposedly only available for export markets; a few UK models were so fitted although it was not publicly announced until the introduction of the Series III.

5.3-litre

Anti-pollution features on the Series II V12 engines included air injection and exhaust gas recirculation, easily identifiable by a second series of pipes running into the inlet manifold and a large air pump situated where the air conditioning idle pulley is normally. Despite this, power output remained the same at this time.

The big change to the V12 engine came in May 1975 with the introduction of fuel injection, providing better economy, 14 per cent more power and reduced pollution. Based on a design made for Jaguar by Bosch with the help of Lucas, the fuel injection system raised power output to

285bhp at 5750rpm. For more details, see *Carburettors & Fuel Injection* (page 93). Coinciding with the arrival of fuel injection, V12 engines received a new rear main-bearing side seal along with a harder crankshaft and greater bearing clearance.

From September 1978 V12 engines had a revised fixing for the oil dipstick tube as the previous type had been found to come loose.

Series III

3.4-litre

The 3.4-litre installation at first remained exactly as on the Series II models. At engine number 8A.86791, however, the interference fit between the head and tappet guide was increased by 0.0125mm, as cam follower guides had been tending to come loose. From January 1980 the engine mounting spacer (part C30721) was deleted to provide better under-bonnet clearance. From September 1984 all engines were provided with a Sursulpha hardened crankshaft (at engine number 8A.15562).

4.2-litre

All 4.2-litre installations in the Series III bodyshell were with fuel injection. The Series III variant developed 205bhp (DIN) at 5000rpm, with torque up from 222lb ft to 236lb ft. Engines received a new air cleaner arrangement to cut down intake noise levels and a fuel cut-off on the overrun (see *Carburettors & Fuel Injection*, page 93). Compression ratio was 8.7:1 through the use of E-type 9.0:1 compression pistons (later cutaway-skirt pistons) and the extra space taken by bigger inlet valves (1⅜in instead of 1¼in). Inlet valves were opened at 22° BTDC instead of 17°.

As on the 3.4-litre engine, the interference fit between the head and the tappet guide was increased by 0.0125mm from engine number 8L.86791, because cam follower guides were coming loose. At the end of 1979 slotted waterways were introduced between the cylinder bores, corresponding with additional waterways in the cylinder head itself, to provide increased coolant transfer between block and head. Fitting later blocks with an earlier head necessitates drilling the head to match the block waterways.

From January 1980 the engine mounting (part C30721) was deleted to provide better under-bonnet clearance. From August 1981 all 4.2-litre engines were fitted with an oil cooler along with a new plastic 18in diameter viscous-coupled cooling fan similar to the one used on V12 engines. Also, from engine number 8L.99605, an improved finish to the cylinder bores (called Plateau) became a feature. From September 1984 (at engine number 8L.167200) a Sursulpha hardened crankshaft was provided, as on the 3.4.

A very late model Series III 4.2-litre engine bay. This engine shows the shape of the fuel injector rail as a single tube; earlier Series IIIs had a continuous loop system. This car also shows the later ballasted coil, not used on earlier Series IIIs, and the yellow plastic cooling fan that replaced a black-painted metal fan midway through Series III production. Simplified exhaust manifold heat shields now no longer have slots and ducting to remove hot air over the engine, and there is a revised radiator expansion tank. This engine is also equipped with cruise control, hence the bellows arrangement and cabling showing below the expansion tank.

Pre-HE fuel-injected V12 engine bay, correct in every detail. Offside gearbox dipstick position indicates the GM400 automatic gearbox (cars with the Model 12 Borg Warner auto 'box had the dipstick on the nearside, as on six-cylinder models). Ignition amplifier is now on the radiator top rail, along with the fuel injection amplifier. As this is a very late Series II car, the battery does not have the cooling fan arrangement.

One of the very last Series III V12 engines, showing catalyst controls and ABS equipment. Also seen is later HE fuel injection with one-piece fuel rail, variable pressure-operated fuel pressure regulators at the end of the rail instead of in the centre, and different style and installation of ignition amplifier on left-hand side of inlet manifold. Post-1987 outer/inner wing joins have U-shaped covering in rubber, not plastic.

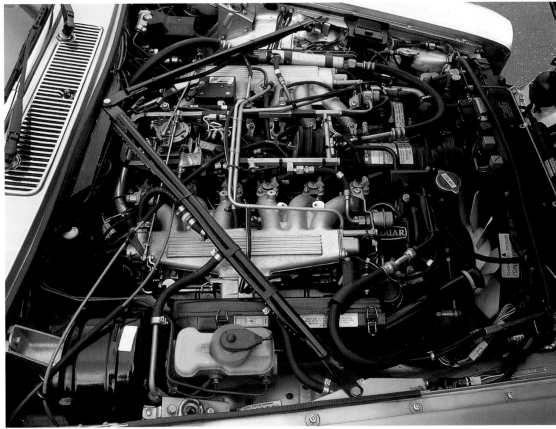

5.3-litre

The greatest change to the V12 engine came in 1981 with the introduction of the revised HE (High Efficiency) version. Michael May from Antipollution Industrial Research developed a revised cylinder head design (known as the Fireball). The head was of split-level design with two vertical valves in a compact, specially-machined combustion chamber allowing the use of flat-top pistons. All this meant less weight and lower operating temperatures, which led to better fuel economy. In practice consumption improved from under 15mpg to nearly 20mpg.

With the combustion chamber on two levels, the inlet valves were lower and closer to the pistons, and the exhaust valves were on a higher level. Tangential grooves ran from the inlet valve seat to the exhaust so that as the piston neared top dead centre, mixture was squeezed between the piston and inlet valves, creating what Jaguar called 'squish'. The mixture swirled around violently, ensuring much more efficient burning. Other changes were a new amplifier of higher power, twin coil ignition, a new Lucas digital electronic fuel injection system and a compression ratio increase from 10.0:1 to 12.5:1.

From about August 1986, at engine number 7P.55762, the V12 was fitted with revised sparking plug leads with a different angle on leads 1A, 1B and 6A to improve fitting and accessibility. In October 1986 a new full-flow oil cooling system was introduced to improve efficiency, with revisions to the cooler and external and internal oil pipes. This occurred at VIN 461921 (engine 7P.56372) for all markets except Germany.

As late as May 1989 the factory decided to replace the rope seal previously used for the rear main oil seal on V12 engines with the one-piece type used on the AJ6 engine. This necessitated a revised cylinder block from engine number 7P.02073, fitted to cars from VIN 481485.

For the 1990 model year, Jaguar made catalytic converters standard for the UK market, unless a customer specified otherwise. This necessitated several changes to the layout, including the use of two Lambda sensors (one for each cylinder bank) and a different engine management ECU.

The compression ratio was changed in February 1990 to 11.5:1 to enable leaded or unleaded fuel to be used. From April 1990 engine number suffixes changed so that the last letter of the engine number suffix was used to denote the emissions type and not the grade of piston (for example, 7P.63107 – SF).

In the 1991 model year the NGK sparking plug type was changed for V12 engines from BR7 EFS to BR7 EF. The new plugs featured a vee-groove in the central electrode, providing the benefits of lower voltage and better igniting.

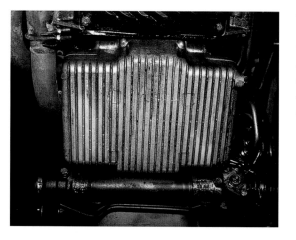

Comparison of very early Series I 4.2-litre sump with fins (left) and later Series I 4.2-litre smooth sump (below left) that continued throughout Series II/III production.

Front sump areas show earlier finned version for a car without air conditioning (left) and the later version for a car with air conditioning (below left), the latter view showing the spigot to hold the revised alternator mounting bracket.

Carburettors & Fuel Injection

XK engines with carburettors were the norm on all Series I models, and virtually all Series II cars until late on, with the introduction of the fuel-injected version initially for the US market; very few injected cars escaped on to the UK market. All Series III cars were fuel injected except for 3.4-litre models. On the V12, only Series I models had carburettors; later cars were fuel-injected.

Carburettor systems

Both the 4.2-litre and 2.8-litre Series I engines used twin SU HD8 carburettors for the home and European markets. The units were finished to a polished alloy state with black plastic dashpot tops. Prior to the introduction of the AED (Automatic Enriching Device), all six-cylinder engines were fitted with a cold-start carburettor instead of a conventional choke. Air conditioned cars had a petrol cooler to prevent fuel vaporisation.

The inlet manifold supposedly had a black 'crackle' finish on all models, but many of the very early engines had a conventional alloy finish, as found on other '60s Jaguar XK engines.

Twin Zenith Stromberg 175 CD carburettors were fitted for the US market because of emissions controls. These carburettors had cast dashpots embossed with the name and number, again with black dashpot tops. Manifolding was the same type as used on the SU-equipped models.

In all cases a single air cleaner was used with a paper element. The air cleaner body, with a bevelled end to the trumpet intake, was painted 'crackle' silver. The relevant photographs show Twin SU HD8 carburettor system, with the electric starting carburettor between the two SUs. Original air cleaner sticker shows the various readings, and at right-hand rear of the air cleaner is the engine breather inlet blank (black in colour) only required for certain overseas markets. Original red tabs on the float chambers show the correct needles to be used.

Two of the four Stromberg 175 CD carburettors used on early V12 engines. This car has no air injection system, which featured only on a few export models and some of the very last UK carburettor models. Air cleaner finish on a few of the very first cars was silver 'crackle', but black is usual.

Carburation on 3.4-litre XJ6 Series II clearly shows the AED (Automatic Enrichment Device) and emission control system, with engine breathing ducted into the carburettors. These are the later SU HS8 carburettors, also used on post-1970 Series I six-cylinder engines. Inlet manifold finish changed from natural alloy to 'crackle' black late in Series I production.

the changes in style and shape of air cleaners throughout the era of Series I, II and III, including the change to a gloss black paint finish for Series II models. On early 2.8-litre engines (from chassis number C.31422) a new filter was used with a neoprene flared end. Dealers were asked to cut off the existing flare on older cars and fit the neoprene replacement.

From October 1969 a modified inlet manifold (part C.31975) was fitted to the 2.8-litre engines, shortened at the front to provide improved access for distributor contact-breaker point adjustment.

In March 1970, SU HS8 carburettors were standardised on all six-cylinder cars with a revised AED for cold starting. This was situated under the rear carburettor with an air-pressure switch in the

Later version of Series II six-cylinder, showing revised SU HIF carburettors incorporating an integrated float chamber and different plastic screw caps on the dashpot tops. Note the fuel cooler pipe across the back of the carburettors used on air conditioning models, and the in-line fuel filter in the foreground. All Series IIs had a black air cleaner finish.

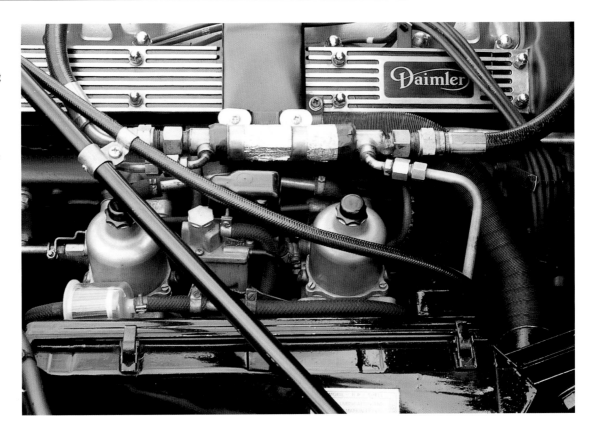

Fuel injection as fitted to Series III six-cylinder cars and a few very late Series IIs. All had black finished inlet manifolding and later models like this had the single tubular style of fuel rail (with a loop of thinner diameter on earlier Series IIIs). Blue plastic sealing plug on air flow meter is an anti-tamper feature, often missing nowadays. An extra air valve (just in front of the coil) was fitted only to cars with air conditioning, to increase engine idle speed when the compressor engaged.

pump circuit. This modification also applied to the 3.4-litre engines when they became available.

On the Series I V12 engines four carburettors were used, of the Stromberg emission-controlled 175 CD type as fitted to the US-specification 4.2-litre engines. It was not possible to fit SUs because of their height. The carburettors were placed outside the engine's 60° vee formation, two on each side. Throttle linkages from the rear pair of carburettors were connected to an alloy capstan system, which sat on a turret bolted to the vee of the engine block.

Two air cleaners (one per side) were fitted to Series I V12s and had a 'crackle' silver finish on the first few hundred cars, but black paint thereafter. The air cleaner bodies were joined to the

Pre-HE fuel-injected V12 configuration (with air conditioning), showing later position for injection amplifier on top of radiator rail.

Later HE V12 fuel injection system, as used until the end of production except for cars fitted with a catalytic converter.

elongated trumpet air intakes by convoluted rubber joints and the trumpets terminated in bevelled rubber ends.

With the arrival of the Series II cars very little changed initially. All six-cylinder cars received a new air cleaner assembly, reshaped because of the exhaust-heated air intake system (see *Exhaust System*, page 98). During Series II production, in May 1976, the existing HS type carburettors were replaced by a new HIF type (Horizontal Integral Floatchamber), which gave automatic adjustment of mixture strength according to the change in

General arrangement of fuel pumps and allied pipework on Series I and early Series II six-cylinder models, within the spare wheel well area up to the introduction of the submersible fuel pumps in the tanks. The warning legend was also fitted to Series I models from the introduction of the V12 engine in 1972 and all subsequent six-cylinder cars. In the centre is the electric aerial unit.

Altered fuel pump arrangement for Series II fuel-injected six-cylinder cars and all V12 injected models. It shows the twin electronic three-way valves controlling fuel return to the tanks, and earlier style roller cell Bosch fuel pump with three-way air bleed valve adjacent to the pump. The fuel filter at this time was remote, in the engine bay.

Series III fuel pump arrangement, with a single electronic three-way valve controlling supply to the pumps. The fuel return valves are now situated at the back of each rear wheelarch. The three-way air bleed valve is now moved to the front of the boot area adjacent to the fuel filter as the fuel pipe passes behind the rear axle.

temperature. This change was effective on 4.2-litre models from engine number 8L.262204.

It is known that 20 of the original V12-engined XJ Coupés left the factory with carburettors, but the rest of these cars were fuel-injected.

Fuel Injection

It was not until May 1975 that Jaguar started to fit fuel injection systems on its cars, at first only for the V12-engined cars as a result of development work for the forthcoming launch of the XJ-S, which was fuel-injected from the start.

The fuel injection system, later to be called the D-Jetronic system, was based on a design made by Bosch but revised specifically for the Jaguar applications by Lucas. Fuel was injected directly into the inlet manifolds and the result was a pretty impressive 285bhp (DIN) at 5750rpm.

The alloy-finished Bosch electronic control unit was placed in the boot. Fuel was supplied under pressure at 28psi to the injector nozzles, via a filter, and surplus pressure was released by a reg-

ulator valve and returned to the tanks. Fuel metering was regulated by a Lucas electronic control unit, in the engine bay alongside the amplifier, in response to four control units. One was a temperature sensor adjusting the fuel delivery from the injectors as required for the warm-up period. Another controlled air temperature in normal running. At the manifold side of the throttle control a pressure sensor determined demand on the engine. Lastly, a throttle switch both indicated throttle position and provided enrichment under acceleration.

Fuel injection arrived with the 4.2-litre Series III model. However a few Series II injected cars 'escaped' from the factory, although a total is not known. The adoption of fuel injection resulted in 19 per cent more power, with torque up from 221lb ft to 236lb ft. The system was the Lucas/Bosch L-Jetronic sealed fuel injection system and a new air cleaner system was fitted to cut down intake roar. The air cleaner had a foam insert and was finished in black with its trumpet running underneath the radiator top rail.

Fuelling Systems

There was a bewildering array of fuel pump arrangements. All Series I six-cylinder cars plus early Series IIs had two single-action SU contact-breaker fuel pumps situated in the spare wheel well of the boot. Later Series II cars from 1977 had submerged fuel pumps fitted in the tanks in the old location for the fuel gauge sender units, which were moved to behind each tail lamp assembly for ease of access. This arrangement carried on for 3.4-litre carburettor Series III cars. Fuel-injected six-cylinder Series II and III cars had one Bosch pump in the boot with two non-return valves located in the rear wheelarches and a three-way valve to draw fuel from the tanks. Complaints about noise from the pumps led in October 1979 to the addition of padding pieces of shaped black rubber between the pump bodies and the boot floor for six-cylinder cars.

The Series I V12 and carburettor-equipped Series II V12s had two double-action SU pumps with two solenoids to each pump body. Unusually the right pump was fed from the left fuel tank and vice versa. V12 pumps carried pre-formed sound-deadening from the start, initially with a yellow foam covering but later a plastic base surround. Two fuel non-return valves were also fitted underneath the boot shut panel on Series I V12s and Series II V12s with carburettors. Fuel-injected Series II and Series III V12s had only one Bosch fuel pump, plus a three-way valve inside the boot well. On Series III V12s the fuel non-return valves were situated at the back of the rear wheelarches.

Fuel lines were of the mild steel type with braided hose connections. Initially the in-line fuel filter was of the conventional bowl type, as used on other '60s Jaguars, and was fitted to the offside inner wing. With the introduction of air conditioning, however, the fuel filter moved to the boot, mounted in the rear right-hand corner of the spare wheel well. This was the position adopted for all Series I cars from December 1970. A fuel shut-off valve was also fitted, dependent on chassis number. For Series II models the in-line fuel filter, of the totally disposable type, returned to the engine bay, but with the introduction of injection to the six-cylinder cars it ended up back in the boot again.

Because of the heat generated by the V12 engine, a recirculating fuel system had to be devised to prevent evaporation of fuel in the under-bonnet area. This is the reason for the use of fuel non-return valves even on the carburettor V12 engines.

At the very end of Series III V12 production an evaporative emissions control system was fitted from VIN 486831. The system was designed to prevent fuel vapour, which consists mainly of

Fuel filter on early Series I models was mounted on offside inner wing until chassis number 1L.66012. Thereafter a conventional glass bowl type filter was fitted in the boot area.

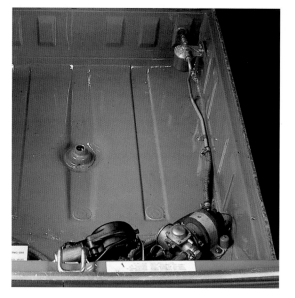

Later Series I and early Series II models had this type of blue steel bowl type filter (with paper disposable element) fitted in the boot up to the introduction of submersible fuel pumps at chassis number 2T.15026.

Series III spare wheel well, showing the bleed valve assembly adjacent to the fuel filter at the back, as fitted to all six-cylinder and V12 models.

hydrocarbons, escaping into the atmosphere. The components were an evaporative loss flange (fitted to the fuel tank), pressure vacuum-relief valve with vacuum-operated by-pass valve, charcoal canister (under the offside front wing), purge control valve, purge air port (on the charcoal canister), purge port (on the induction manifold), electrical connection to the ECU, and a revised type of induction manifold. A similiar system was adopted much earlier from Series I production for cars destined for certain overseas countries with specific emissions regulations.

Cooling System

Engine cooling for the XJ6 Series I was significantly improved over previous models. There was a larger 3in impeller on the water pump, combined with a smaller pulley to ensure faster rotation at 1.25 times engine speed. The by-pass hose, which on the 2.8-litre acted as the main water feed to the engine, was 1in larger and there were water transfer holes in the cylinder head gasket (larger on the exhaust side). All these changes combined to eliminate the need for a conventional water gallery for the 4.2-litre engines.

A cross-flow radiator system was used with separate header tank, finished in gloss black, fitted to the nearside inner wing on 4.2s and above the radiator on 2.8s. Series I cars had a four-row radiator core, Series II cars a two-row core. On automatic transmission models a heat transfer pipe was fitted as a split from the bottom hose.

In March 1970 the factory had to alter the shape of the bottom water hose, to stop it being rubbed through by the fan belt when on full adjustment. At the same time the upper radiator fan cowl used on air conditioned cars was standardised for all 4.2-litre models.

From March 1972 all cars without air conditioning received a revised radiator filler cap rated at 13psi pressure instead of the previous 4psi. At the end of Series II production, from engine numbers 8L.51581 (4.2) and 8A.7841 (3.4), pressure caps were revised to 15psi. April 1981 saw the introduction of the brown plastic radiator header tank that was used for the remainder of production, still fitted to the front nearside inner wing.

For the V12 coolant capacity increased to four gallons. Coolant temperature was controlled by an engine-driven 17in Torquatrol viscous-coupled fan, plus an Airscrew electric fan and two thermostats. A black-finished oil cooler was also fitted to the base of the radiator.

With the advent of the 'sealed bulkhead' arrangement on the Series II cars, air conditioning pipes were bolted directly on to the expansion valve and evaporator outlets. This expansion valve and outlets were part of the heater box fixed to the inside of the car and protruded through the bulkhead, sealed with mastic. Connections for the heater matrix were also part of this unit.

Radiator top rail looking from the extreme front, on Series I/II 4.2 cars without air conditioning (left) and with it (below). With air conditioning, there is an extension too for the condenser.

Radiator top rail on earlier V12 models (right) incorporates the air bleed valve tap and appropriate circular legend. On later V12 models (far right) the bleed tap is replaced by a bleed rail; note the air conditioning condenser position. Radiator foam padding (below) should be fitted to all models but is often discarded.

This is the transmission fluid cooler – a tube within the lower engine cooling system transfer pipe. All cars had this drain plug for coolant until its deletion midway through 1986.

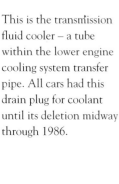

Heater valves as fitted to a six-cylinder Series I car (far left) and any Series II/III car (middle left). On the earlier model it comes off the back of the inlet manifold, supported on a bracket; the same valve was used on Series I V12s, but located by the battery box. Coolant drain tap (near left) as fitted to six-cylinder Series I engine blocks until engine numbers 7G.2488 (2.8) and 7L.4383 (4.2). Later models had a blanking bolt.

Screenwash components

The windscreen washer reservoir on the Series I models was an opaque plastic bottle with a large grey screw cap. The bottle was attached via a black metal bracket to the battery carrier. The system was activated by an electric pump (with a grey finish) situated under the bulkhead or in the centre of the engine bay.

With the introduction of the V12 engine, space was obviously at a premium. So the washer bottle was reduced in size to a rectangular shape, with a small yellow press-on cap, and fitted to the forward edge of the nearside inner wing, at the side of the coolant header tank.

This arrangement was retained on all models until the Series III, when the reservoir was re-sited under the front of the nearside wing with only the filler visible in the engine bay. The new filler had a translucent plastic press-on cap.

In all cases green translucent piping was used for washer bottle connections.

Exhaust System

All the Series XJ saloons, regardless of specification and engine size, used a twin-pipe system throughout. The exhaust system, like many other aspects of the car, had been developed to eliminate noise and make the car as refined as possible.

The exhaust manifold arrangement was conventional Jaguar on Series I six-cylinder models. Two three-branch iron castings, both of which were attractively vitreous-enamelled in black, had four-stud fixings to each flexible downpipe. The twin downpipes were then siamesed to eliminate any extraneous engine reverberations. The system then separated again into two pipes running along the underside of the floorpan to two small oval silencer boxes ahead of the rear subframe. The pipes then lifted over the rear axle and curved outwards to two larger circular silencer boxes. Straight chromed pipes were fitted to the extreme ends of both exhausts and emerged through holes in the rear body valance – a very unusual arrangement for the day. The six-cylinder cars used 1⅞in bore exhaust piping. Asbestos heat shields were fitted above the forward silencers to restrict heat transfer to the cabin.

In mid-1969 the straight chromed tailpipe trims fitted to both 2.8-litre and 4.2-litre models were changed to an S shape, a deliberate and necessary alteration in view of complaints from customers about exhaust fumes entering the interior of the car. The reason for this was that exhaust fumes were being dragged aerodynamically along the sides of the car and up through open windows. Amazingly the new pipes eliminated this trait.

Very little changed with the introduction of the V12-engined Series I XJs. The exhaust manifold arrangement was very similar although, of course, there were actually four three-branch castings. They were not vitreous-enamelled, probably because they were essentially hidden from view. Exhaust manifolds were covered with bolt-on alloy shields. The exhaust pipe run was also different from the six-cylinder cars and was a twin system for its complete length. Exhaust pipe bore was increased to 2in and the front pipes to the first silencer boxes were double-skinned. To withstand the tremendous heat generated through the exhaust, heat shielding was fitted along the whole length of the floorpan underside.

Although this is a modern exhaust system, it shows the essentially correct style and fitting of the Series I system. The two pipes have a siamese section (below left) and then spread out into the silencer boxes (below). Later Series I cars were given a shield between the gearbox and the siamese section. All six-cylinder models after chassis number 1L.32831 had the two downpipes merging into one, avoiding the siamese arrangement.

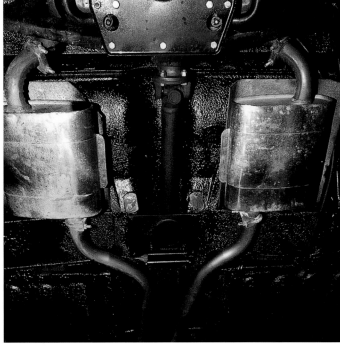

The Series I exhaust system showing the pipes and silencers as they emerge from the rear cage, looking backwards to where the pipes pass through the rear body valance.

With the introduction of the long-wheelbase models, the straight-run sections of the exhaust pipes were increased in length by 4in for those models. All systems by this time used the S-shaped tailpipes with unflared ends. All exhausts were of mild steel construction – stainless steel systems were never available from the factory.

In March 1970 all six-cylinder cars received new emissions exhaust manifolds. These were no longer vitreous-enamelled and had tappings in the top to enable heat shields to be bolted on. The rear manifolds had casting changes and tappings to bolt the heater duct pipe to the AED system, plus a larger tapping that combined to hold the heat shield and provide exhaust gas recirculation. To accommodate the ducting, a cut-out was designed into the exhaust cam cover and this remained a feature on all six-cylinder engines throughout the remainder of production, even after the removal of the ducting from the engines of subsequent models.

Little changed for the Series IIs, particularly on the V12s. For six-cylinder models, however, Jaguar applied new technology in the form of ducting to transfer heat from the exhaust manifolds back over the engine to meet up with the air filter inlet. Initially this was seen on cars destined for North America, where emissions controls were becoming more stringent, but later it found its way on to all cars. The ducting, which allowed heated air to enter the engine, thereby reducing emissions in cold weather, was always in a satin black finish, while the manifold surround was polished high-grade stainless steel.

For both 4.2-litre and 3.4-litre engines on Series II cars, Jaguar also eliminated the old flexible exhaust downpipes and replaced them with a merged 23in-long section of double-skinned piping. This then separated to run the length of the car with the twin silencers as used on the Series I models.

In May 1978, with the adoption of fuel injection on the XK power unit, catalytic converters were fitted to some export models and were available by special request on English cars.

With the launch of the Series III saloons, the same exhaust systems were carried over from the Series II models except for a slight trim change on the now stainless steel S-shaped tailpipes. Now finishing in a flare, these were lengthened to clear the deeper rear bumpers, and continued in this form on all cars through to the end of production. Also there were differences in the way the exhaust system connected together; the joint between the

Series I/II intermediate silencer with correct heat shielding and the U bolt holding the slide fitting where it connects to the over-axle pipe. With the introduction of Series III models this U bolt connection was replaced by a flange fitting.

Early Series I chromed straight tailpipe (right) is now quite rare to find. Later Series I and all Series II models used the 'S' bend style of chromed exhaust trim (far right) with an unflared end.

All Series IIIs used a similar tailpipe (right), but it is longer – to clear the extended bumpers – and has a flared end. Catalyst and downpipe arrangement (far right) on the very last V12-engined cars.

intermediate silencer and over-axle exhaust pipe now became a bolted-together flange fitting, as opposed to a male and female slot connection.

Exhaust mounting brackets in the rear axle cage changed in both style and position throughout the life of all models. Earliest Series Is had a single nut and bolt holding the circular support bracket to the roof of the axle cage. Later Series Is and many Series IIs had essentially the same round bracket, but now it was held to the roof of the cage by two bolts going into captive nuts. Series IIIs had a pressed steel U-shaped bracket also attached to the roof of the cage via bolts and captive nuts. In all cases the outer metal section contained a correspondingly shaped rubber bush and the appropriate internal fibre insulator.

From February 1990 all V12 engines came available with the option of catalytic converters, which were already standard on most export cars but not compulsory for the UK. The exhaust assembly was different, with intermediate pipes and downpipes into which were inserted two catalytic converters, each one astride the engine oil sump. Heat shielding was also provided to suit the new exhaust installation because of the increased temperatures reached in the system.

Transmission

Over the years the gearboxes used by Jaguar for the XJ have varied significantly. Manual gearboxes were relatively common for Series I and II models, much less so on early Series III cars and never available on later models. Automatic transmissions were by far the more popular option for XJ Series models in general and the two major systems used were manufactured for Jaguar by Borg Warner and General Motors.

With the introduction of the Series I XJ6, both manual and automatic transmissions were available. Both 2.8 and 4.2 cars used exactly the same manual gearbox, the conventional four-speed all-synchromesh type as fitted by Jaguar in other saloons from 1965 onwards. For the XJ the helix angle of the constant mesh gears was increased to 34° to reduce noise levels. The bell housings looked the same but were in fact different. The 2.8-litre model had 104 teeth on the ring gear and a Mark 2 style inertia starter. The 4.2-litre had 133 teeth and a pre-engaged starter located on hollow dowels. If the wrong bell housing is fitted to an engine there will be difficulty in meshing the starter motor.

From March 1969 the gearbox oil filler plug was moved to the right-hand side of the gearbox from the left for all models. This effectively increased the oil capacity by ½ pint to 4½ pints. At the same time, from engine number 7L.1630, 4.2-litre cars received an improved type of clutch unit incorporating a higher-rated diaphragm spring to prevent clutch slip at high mileage.

The 'Standard' saloon did not feature overdrive, but on the other models the option of the Laycock de Normanville overdrive unit was available. It functioned on top gear only and was operated by a neat sliding switch on top of the black gear knob. The gear lever itself was chromed with a black plastic gaiter.

The Salisbury rear axle was of the hypoid bevel gear type with a ratio, where overdrive was fitted, of 3.77:1 for the 4.2-litre engine and 4.55:1 on 2.8-litre cars. For non-overdrive cars the ratios were 3.31:1 and 4.27:1 respectively.

Where automatic transmission was fitted, two different types of Borg Warner 'box were used according to engine size. For the smaller 2.8-litre

engine (for the whole period of production) the Borg Warner Type 35 was fitted in conjunction with a 4.09:1 rear axle ratio. This was arguably a slighter better 'box than the old Borg Warner Model 8 transmission used on the larger-engined cars with a 3.54:1 rear axle ratio. Both were conventional three-speed gearboxes but on the Type 35 two 'Drive' positions were fitted, then a relatively new feature for automatic transmission on the British market.

Regardless of the type of automatic transmission used, gear selection was by a chromed T-bar (with black side screw) on the centre console. Black plastic with a white legend was used for the quadrant identification, set into a moulded fibreboard surround again finished in black.

From the end of 1969, however, the Model 8 unit was replaced on 4.2-litre engines by the Borg Warner Model 12, also having the two 'Drive' positions. This was a much more sophisticated gearbox more suited to the refinement of the XJ6, and it also improved acceleration. This change took place from chassis numbers 1L.4988 (right-hand drive) and 1L.57296 (left-hand drive).

For the new transmission the old throttle-

Series I/II manual gear lever had a chromed stalk and quite an elaborate knob, incorporating the overdrive switch when applicable.

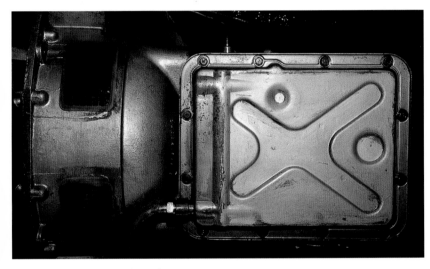

Underside sump styles with Borg Warner automatic transmission, on a Series I 4.2-litre XJ6 with the Model 12 gearbox (top) and a Series II/III car with the Model 65 or 66 gearbox (above).

Sump pan on the later GM 400 automatic transmission. Earlier versions had a slightly shallower sump.

cable kick-down system was replaced by a microswitch for full kick-down and a vacuum control system, consisting of a pipe conveying engine manifold depression to a vacuum servo mounted at the rear of the transmission, for part-throttle changes. Hydraulic line pressures were therefore partly controlled by manifold depression, with smoothness of gear changes being adjusted by a screw located in the servo unit. The original vacuum unit was replaced with a smaller version with a shorter pushrod to the throttle valve in April 1971.

For many months after the installation of the Model 12 transmission, the official handbooks supplied with the cars showed incorrectly that there was a detent between the engagement of D1 and D2. Later handbooks were suitably amended when reprinted.

On all 4.2-litre cars a limited slip differential was supposedly standard, but it was known for cars to 'escape' from the factory without this.

From May 1969 cars destined for the US and Canada received the 3.31:1 rear axle ratio on automatic transmission 4.2-litre models and similarly the 2.8-litre for the Canadian market had the 4.09:1 ratio.

With the introduction of the XJ12 in 1972, the new Borg Warner Model 12 gearbox was fitted, totally re-engineered internally but externally looking the same as the six-cylinder equivalent. The unit was much stronger, to take the tremendous torque generated by the 12-cylinder engine, and also much smoother in operation, as had already been found in the 4.2-litre cars. The Salisbury rear axle had a new ratio of 3.31:1 (as then fitted to 4.2-litre models) and had a limited-slip differential as standard.

From the introduction of the new 3.4-litre engine for the Series II XJ6, the manual transmission was redesigned with the bottom ratio lowered from 2.93:1 to 3.25:1, which applied at the same time to 4.2-litre cars as well. Overdrive was always standard on 3.4-litre Series II manual cars.

Changes made to automatic transmission systems on the Series II models included the installation in all six-cylinder models of another new Borg Warner automatic transmission, the Type 65, which provided an even smoother gear change than the previous Model 12. With the Model 65 'box, the construction of the unpainted casing changed from aluminium to cast iron.

Late in 1975 the final drive ratio on V12 cars was amended to 3.07:1 from 3.31:1, giving 24.7mph per 1000rpm in top gear (instead of 22.9mph). This not only gave the V12 a genuine 100mph at only 4050rpm, but contributed to improved smoothness and refinement.

A significant transmission change was made in April 1977 when all V12-engined cars received

Drive trains of a Series I 4.2-litre car (above left) and a late V12 with catalyst (above).

the General Motors GM400 three-speed automatic 'box. Although already established as a superior and smoother unit, its main advantage in the V12 was its capability to handle the vast amount of torque well.

With the introduction of the Series III XJ models came a new five-speed manual transmission, which was based on the British Leyland Rover gearbox used in the SD1 saloon. There was a new casing (although still retaining the BL logo on the side!) along with a stronger 77mm layshaft, plus bigger bearings and altered ratios to cope with the additional power of the Jaguar engine. The design and use of this gearbox had previously been carried out for the Police Specification XJs. The fifth (overdrive) gear gave 25.8mph per 1000rpm. The chromed gear lever had a black top with white legend for gear positions and a black leather gaiter fitted to the new-style black vinyl centre console surround.

Also with the introduction of the Series III models came the option of the Econocruise speed control system (cruise control), on automatic transmission cars only. It became standard on Jaguar Sovereign V12 models and Daimlers from the 1984 model year. Operational controls inside the car amounted to another black rocker switch mounted behind the selector quadrant, necessi-

tating a restyled and lengthened surround and plastic legend. This rocker switch controlled the 'On/Off' mode of the cruise control and the 'Resume' facility to re-adopt a chosen speed previously disengaged. The 'Set' control was a black push button at the side of the left-hand steering column stalk. Although quite sophisticated, the system gave very little trouble. It was based on just four switches: the 'Set' switch on the stalk, a brake switch operated from the brake pedal to disengage the system when the foot brake was applied, the master switch on the console and the gear inhibitor, which prevented operation of the system except in 'Drive'.

The system's control unit was situated under the facia on the left-hand side (right-hand drive cars). The speed transducer on the early cars controlled the speed of the car via the accelerator cables and an actuator controlling the pulses from the control unit, allowing manifold vacuum to pull open the throttle. This transducer comprised a sensor bolted to the rear axle cage (in front of the differential nose) and magnets attached to the propshaft. The vacuum unit (or actuator) to control engine speed was bolted to the left-hand inner wing on six-cylinder cars and in the centre of the vee, just behind the air conditioning compressor, on V12 engines. Where air conditioning

Propshaft centre bearing mount seen in early (above) and late (above right) forms. The change occurred at chassis number 2T.13518, late in Series II production.

was not fitted this item was fastened to a bridge across the vee. With the introduction of an electronic speedometer, the speed sensing was taken direct from the back of the speedometer, so dispensing with the need for the transducer.

From April 1982 the automatic transmission selector was amended on all cars, with the detent relocated from between D and D2 to between D and N, making for easier operation. This necessitated a slight change to the legend on the black plastic top of the quadrant.

Coinciding with the above change, the six-cylinder cars received another new automatic transmission unit, this time the Borg Warner Model 66, also of aluminium construction. Predating this (in 1981) the decision was taken to drop the manual transmission from all Jaguar saloons. Fewer than 15 per cent of customers for Series I and II models had ever specified a manual transmission, and, significantly, this proportion had dropped further with the Series III models. Interestingly, Jaguar still eschews manual transmission nowadays, even for its sports cars.

In October 1986 a revised GM400 automatic transmission was fitted to V12 cars to overcome oil ejection problems under extreme operating conditions. The new transmission incorporated a deeper sump and revised dipstick assembly (with

brown handle) from engine number 7P.56895.

No further changes took place until May 1989, when the GM400 transmission in V12s was recalibrated to improve response, particularly on kickdown. Change speeds were amended to: first to second, 53/60mph at full throttle; second to third, 94/99mph at full throttle; third to second, 96/108mph upon kickdown; second to first, 44/50mph upon kickdown.

As far as clutches were concerned for the manual transmission models, all 3.4-litre and 4.2-litre cars used a 9.5in diaphragm Borg & Beck clutch assembly. For the later Leyland five-speed gearbox, however, a roller thrust bearing was used instead of the carbon type on the earlier cars. For the 2.8-litre engines an 8.5in Borg & Beck clutch assembly was fitted, of exactly the same type as used on the previous 240 saloons.

The propshaft centre bearing and mounts changed throughout production. On all Series I cars and many Series IIs this assembly was made up of one large carrier plate spanning the transmission tunnel and a second plate bolted to it. Inside were two opposed rubber bushes supporting the propshaft centre bearing. After this a single plate was used with a forward-protruding nose, on to which a new design of self-contained bearing was bolted direct.

Suspension & Steering

Although the XJ6 was considered a very complex and all-new design upon its launch in 1968, in fact most of the mechanical aspects were merely developments of earlier models, refined and adapted as necessary. Checking individual chassis numbers makes it clear that many changes took place over the period of production, and that in some cases some of the very earliest production of a Series would have had similar mechanical components to another Series pre-dating it.

The rear suspension of the XJ6, for example, was virtually identical to the caged layout used on the E-type and Mark X from 1961, and later the S-type and 420 saloons. It was based on unequal length wishbones with fixed-length drive shafts forming the upper wishbones. Heavy tubular transverse links with forged trunnions formed the bottom links, and duplex spring and damper units (four in total) were fitted astride the drive shafts.

Radius arms, of the same style as previous '60s independent rear suspension Jaguars but now of hollow (instead of box section) design, were attached to the main structure via perforated-type pancake rubber bushes. The radius arm safety strap altered from Series I to Series II production by a different size dimension and location point to the floorpan in relation to the radius arm.

The whole of the rear suspension, including the differential and inboard disc brakes, was located in a pressed steel subframe attached to the bodyshell behind the rear seat floor. It was suitably insulated against road noise and shock by Metalastik mountings. The whole system was very efficient in keeping the road wheels constantly in vertical contact with the road and was used on all Series I, II and III XJ models.

At the rear all cars were fitted with 'tie-down' brackets for car transit. On Series I and most Series II models these took the form of a hook fixed to the outer fulcrum pin which ties the lower dampers to the lower wishbone. For later Series II and all Series III models this was replaced by a plate, which went across from the damper fulcrum pin to the lower fulcrum pin at the hub. All types were finished in black.

For the front suspension, coil springs and wishbones were used but incorporating semi-trailing wishbones and an anti-roll bar. Although quite conventional in these respects, the system differed from previous types because anti-dive geometry was incorporated and outboard-mounted dampers were used.

The front suspension was mounted very much as the previous 420G model except that the cross-member in this instance formed a box section member instead of being a forged beam. This sub-frame was attached to the bodywork by rubber Metalastik mountings and located longitudinally by large-diameter rubber trunnions, which had a carefully calculated compliance. The front engine

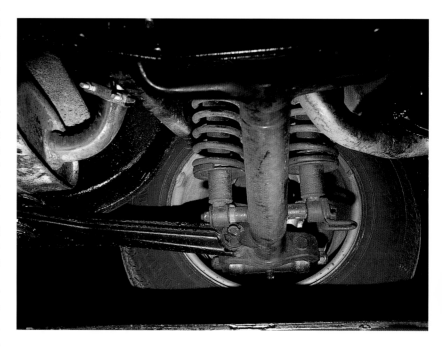

Rear suspension (above) changed very little over the whole period of production, but a detail indicative of an early car is the hoop at the back of the rear damper for a transport tie-down strap. Later a bracket was substituted (left), going across from the hub to the damper fulcrum pin.

Rear radius arm mounting remained the same on all cars, but for the Series II the safety strap changed from a position in line with the radius arm (right) to one predominantly at right angles to it (far right).

The early style of front spring pan (right), which lasted through Series I and Series II XJ production to chassis number 2T.1525, and the later style (far right) fitted to all subsequent models. Latter view also shows the greasable lower ball joint and track rod end.

Rear suspension hub remained unchanged except for the adoption in 1991 of the ABS sensor, seen here entering the hub. From 1990 sealed-for-life hubs were used, with no access for greasing.

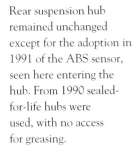

Late Series III car with sealed-for-life lower ball joint and track rod end, respectively introduced in 1987 and early '80s.

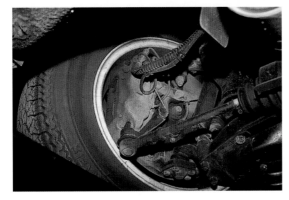

mountings were also fitted to the cross-member, thus eliminating a good deal of engine vibration from the body structure.

By inclining the upper wishbone fulcrum upwards at 3½° to the horizontal and the lower ones downwards at 4°, kingpin angle was effectively altered, reducing the tendency for the front springs to compress under load when the brakes were applied heavily. On braking, the pressure on the wishbones tended to lift the car against the downward forces, giving a 50 per cent anti-dive characteristic.

In line with the above, softer springing was used on the XJ, with a total movement between bump stop and rebound of 7in. An anti-roll bar acting on the bottom wishbones was also fitted and Jaguar chose to fit Girling Monotube dampers outboard of the springs. The dampers were mounted direct to the bodywork via top bushes of expanded polyurethane (with black rubber covers) for better noise insulation. In May 1969 4.2-litre models received stiffer front springs from chassis 1L.2671 (right-hand drive) and 1L.51097 (left-hand drive).

The first use of anti-roll bar drop arms came as a direct link with the previous S-type and 420 models (part C.27781) and applied to XJ6s up to chassis numbers 1G.1098 (right-hand drive) and 1G.50065 (left-hand drive) on 2.8-litre models, and 1L.1370 (right-hand drive) and 1L.50252 (left-hand drive) on 4.2-litre cars. The second stage involved a stronger anti-roll bar drop arm (part C.36887), which was essentially a larger diameter arm. It came in from chassis 1G.1099 to 1G.5047, 1G.50066 to 1G.52313, 1L.13721 to 1L.6945 and 1L50253 to 1L.53559. The same type was fitted to all models until the end of Series III production.

All the mechanical parts of the suspension such as springs, suspension frames, spring pans, anti-roll bar, cross-member, etc, were black. Damper casings were grey.

The only suspension changes necessary for the V12 engine installation from 1972 were uprated and slightly lengthened front springs to accommodate the extra weight – the V12 was 80lb heavier than the XK unit. Springs these days are identifiable by coloured markings, which indicate how many shims should be inserted in the spring pans according to model. These days the same size of spring tends to be supplied for all models, the shims added as necessary to suit engine size and model Series. The markings used therefore cannot be relied upon as always correct.

Stronger spring pans were also used for V12-engined cars but these are not easily identifiable from the six-cylinder type. Also the lower wishbones were altered to compensate for the effective offset of the ventilated front discs. It is therefore not possible to fit a ventilated front disc assembly on to a standard XJ6 upright.

All air conditioned cars used stronger springs and anti-roll bars.

Rack and pinion steering was used on all of these cars. Power assistance applied to all models except on the 'Standard' 2.8-litre Series I, for which it was an extra-cost option.

The brand new rack and pinion system was made for Jaguar by Adwest Engineering and Alford and Adler. The rack was mounted behind the suspension subframe for greater safety and finished in black. The upper steering column, made by AC-Delco, consisted of two parts sleeved together and located by small plastic pins, which would shear under heavy load. Even the casting had a collapsible section.

The lower column section was connected by a universal joint, permitting the column to bend in the event of a crash. There was also a swinging link at the bottom end to accommodate flexing of the cross-member mountings.

The power steering system was a development of the system used on the previous 420G, pressure being supplied at 1100-1250psi from a vane-type pump driven by a belt from the nose of the crankshaft, with a spring-loaded jockey pulley to provide tensioning.

With the Series II models and the 'sealed bulkhead', flexible boots were also fitted to the steering column where it passed through into the engine bay. Part way through Series II production the steering rack and columns were changed. The

length of the valve body was reduced, requiring a correspondingly increased length to the lower steering column. This was to help provide better 'feel' to the steering.

After the introduction of the Series III models, in March 1979, the Alford and Adler power steering rack was changed on all six-cylinder cars to a common type with internal parts, as used on the contemporary Austin Princess and Triumph TR8, taken from the Leyland parts bin.

At the beginning of 1982 modified steering racks with altered lock stops were fitted to V12-engined cars to comply with new European regulations. In February 1982 all models received a revised upper steering column to stop extraneous noises when under load. This was fitted from VIN 336087 and 334145.

For the 1985 model year a new power steering rack without the rack damper grease nipple was used; it also had a new tangential valve and torsion bar. These were fitted to cars from VIN 413000. In February 1990 another new rack was required on cars then fitted with catalytic converters. This was in essence the rack used on Japanese-market models, with forward-facing ports permitting adequate hose clearances.

Correct assembly of the steering rack bush for all models.

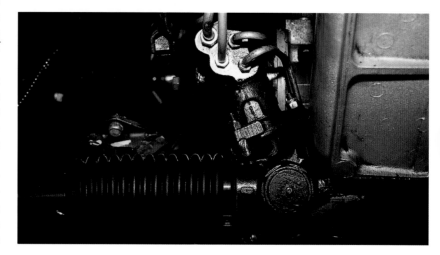

The long-pinion steering rack as fitted to Series I and Series II cars up to chassis number 2T.25108.

Brakes

A quite sophisticated Girling braking system was employed on the XJ6. All-round disc brakes with a dual-line braking system and tandem master cylinder were incorporated.

Initial specification for the Series I was as follows. At the front 11.87in discs were used with ventilated shields in black finish. The three-cylinder calipers, each finished in zinc colour, contained two brake pads, and the two outer pistons were of smaller diameter than the inner one. At the rear 10.38in discs were fitted inboard with a twin-cylinder caliper system, each piston of the same size. A Girling tandem master cylinder with direct-acting servo was employed, the brake pedal acting directly on the master cylinder pushrods. Very early servos were finished in a 'crackle' silver colour with a passivated zinc finish to the master cylinder.

The ratcheted handbrake operated a cable system (which remained the same for all models throughout production, except long-wheelbase cars which had a longer cable) that ran underneath the floorpan to separate calipers fitted above the footbrake calipers in the rear cage. In 1969 a revised handbrake linkage was used with an improved clevis pin arrangement for longer life. A great number of minor changes to brackets and linkages occurred through Series I production, but none affected the handbrake assembly too much and were largely effected for ease of maintenance. The situation stabilised from chassis numbers 1G.10078, 1G.55658, 1L.19359 and 1L.64077.

Around 1978, the handbrake caliper assembly and cable changed during the production period of the last Series IIs. The old method of fixing the end of the handbrake cable to the caliper using a clevis pin was replaced by a soldered nipple on the cable that interlocked with the caliper. The shape of the black handbrake ratchet handle changed slightly for the Series III, having a slightly less rounded form than on the Series I and II models.

At first all XJ6 Series I underbody brake line areas had a protective black plastic covering in the form of a squared-edged U-section conduit, but from July 1970 this was removed, leaving the brake lines open to the elements. At the same time a revised brake fluid reservoir was adopted,

Earlier Series I brake servo and master cylinder, with reservoir and filler behind the servo body. Master cylinder was shared with V12 models during Series I production.

Series I V12 brake servo, set further back (with revised design for reservoir and piping) and subsequently used on all remaining Series I models and Series II cars. Servo finish on Series I V12 was natural metal, probably to differentiate pressure requirement.

Series II brake servo and master cylinder, now much further forward because pedal box arrangement changed. Regardless of engine, all servo bodies were now black. Note revised master cylinder with push-on tops, and correct label for all Series I/II servo styles.

positioned on the inboard side of the booster, instead of at the rear.

Introduction of the V12-engined models brought uprated brakes. Front discs, the same as used on the contemporary E-types, were ventilated (0.94in thick) and of larger diameter (11.18in), with a three-pot caliper. A Kelsey-Hayes brake balance valve was added to guard against rear wheel lock-up under heavy braking. Power assistance came from a Girling Supervac brake servo (with plain metal finish) with an additional reserve tank in black polypropylene fitted under the right-hand front wing.

With the introduction of Series II models ventilated front disc brakes with four-cylinder calipers were standardised on all models regardless of engine size, along with modified pressure differential wiring on the brake system to warn of lack of pressure in one of the brake lines. The rear brake calipers changed in 1977; while they remained interchangeable with the older type, the pistons and seals were not. The earlier calipers were distinguished by a large dust seal, which protruded to a greater degree than the piston itself. The later type has a concertina seal with an easily-visible wire retaining ring. With the advent of an effectively 'sealed bulkhead', the pedal box was fitted with flexible rubber boots as further insulation from mechanical noise. From 1974 brake servo finish changed to shiny black and remained so for the rest of production.

No braking system changes were made for the Series III other than the adoption of anti-squeal bands for the front calipers. From August 1982 all cars had plastic-coated brake pipes throughout and the brake pressure differential warning actuator was deleted.

For the 1991 model year all remaining Series III V12-engined cars were fitted with the Bosch ABS anti-lock braking system as standard. The units were the same as used on the then new XJ40 cars and are interchangeable. This was part of a phased-in programme starting at VIN 483818.

The installation of this Bosch system in the under-bonnet area necessitated the removal of the battery from its previous location to the boot area (see *Boot & Tool Kit*, page 43). The battery space was taken up with the ABS modulator (anodised gold in colour with a black plastic dust cover with 'ABS' printed on) and valve block assembly (with natural alloy finish). This also meant a revised brake pipe layout in the engine compartment with pipes from and to the master cylinder passing over the bulkhead area. Subsequent feed piping also changed, running to the front nearside caliper and then via the front of the car to the offside caliper and along the normal underbody route to the rear.

The ABS Bosch ECU was the same type as on pre-1990 XJ40 models, but not interchangeable

Series III brake servo and master cylinder installation, also applicable to final 12 months of Series II production. Reservoir is now integral with the master cylinder, and labelling revised.

Very late Series III V12 installation, incorporating different piping because of ABS.

Protective plastic channel over the brake pipes underneath the car featured only on early Series I, until chassis number 1L.7230.

due to software amendments; for Series III use it was identified by a purple label. The ECU was security checked by a keyway on the connector. It was mounted in the left-hand side of the footwell and accessed by removal of the side scuttle trim panel at the base of the A post (located with a drain hole facing down to the floorpan). Over-

Series I front disc and three-piston caliper for six-cylinder cars (above) and V12s (above right). Ventilated front discs were adopted for the V12, their extra thickness requiring a spacer block between the two halves of the caliper.

Late model Series III V12 front brake, with symmetrical four-piston caliper and wiring to the ABS sensor.

voltage relays for the ABS system (white case with a green base) were accommodated under the dashboard on the passenger side.

Also beneath the carpet of the front left-side footwell was a lateral acceleration switch. Mercury operated, it monitored and compensated for the vehicle's particular handling characteris-tics and was wired to the ABS warning light on the facia. When ABS was fitted there were sensors for all wheels. The sensor leads entered the engine bay for the front sensors and entered the luggage compartment for the rear sensors. Each sensor connected to the ABS harness via a two-way Bosch connector.

Wheels & Tyres

With the launch of the Series I XJ6 the only wheels offered were traditional 15in steel ones in a silver colour with 6in rims. Chrome-plated rim-bellishers of the snap-fit type were standard on 4.2-litre models but were not fitted to 2.8-litre cars except at extra cost. Hub caps were of the traditional Jaguar style, as on the 240/340 and 420G, with a separate black centre plaque with a silver Jaguar 'growler'; on all Daimler models the hub cap centre plaque contained a silver 'D' insignia.

Tyres had been specially developed by Dunlop in conjunction with Jaguar and were unique to the XJ6. These SP Sport tyres were a derivative of the previous highly successful Dunlop SP radial and had an irregular tread pattern to prevent resonance plus an Aquajet drainage system to clear water quickly from the tread surface. Tyre size was ER70VR-15.

With the introduction of the more powerful V12-engined Jaguars and Daimlers came a new style of wheel and tyre although still retaining the 6in rim width. Dunlop re-developed the existing SP sport tyre with a VR rating, using a nylon casing and steel breaker strip to cope with the car's extra weight. This then became known as the 205/70VR-15 type.

To accompany the new tyres on the V12 there was a new style of ventilated steel wheel with 11

All 2.8-litre Series I models had conventional steel wheels painted silver (below left), with Jaguar style chromed hub caps. Only the 4.2-litre Series I came from the factory with chromed rimbellishers (below), an extra-cost option for cheaper models.

elongated slots to aid brake cooling. The existing snap-on rimbellisher still fitted the new wheel and it remained standard equipment on all models. The hub caps, however, although of exactly the same style as on the earlier cars, were of different proportions as used on the Series III E-types.

Throughout Series I production the ventilated wheels were standard equipment on all V12-engined cars, including Vanden Plas versions, while the earlier wheels remained specified for six-cylinder models. All wheels were silver coloured as standard, but the ventilated type became available in a chromed finish (first seen on the E-type Series III sports car in 1971) as an extra-cost option on any Jaguar or Daimler saloon from April of that year.

There were few changes during Series II production, with chromed wheels still available as an extra-cost option on all models, but never fitted as standard equipment. The original XJ style of steel wheel was dropped so that all models now used the ventilated type. On the 3.4-litre cars, both Jaguar and Daimler, chromed rimbellishers were still not fitted as standard.

From its introduction the XJ-S coupé was equipped with new light alloy GKN Kent wheels incorporating five satin grey segments. These alloy wheels became available at extra cost on Series II XJ saloons but again never featured as standard equipment, although they were specified by many owners, particularly of V12 models, when ordering their cars new.

When the Series III XJ was introduced Jaguar were still using the same Dunlop SP Sport tyres and the ventilated steel wheels painted silver. Gone, though, were the conventional rimbellishers and hub caps, replaced with a new type of integrated stainless steel trim with a matt black finish to the ventilation slot surrounds, to some extent emulating an alloy wheel style. The wheel nuts themselves were now also polished and the wheel trim was held in place by springs under the trim that kept it taut to the wheel.

The trims themselves had a recessed centre section with a prominent domed cap with the usual Jaguar 'growler' or Daimler 'D' on a black background. However, Jaguar marketing, as so many times before with items like coachlines, got to work in an attempt to personalise and differentiate the various models. So, the hub caps were painted differently to suit. On 3.4-litre models the centre section around the wheel nuts was painted all black, for 4.2-litre models a bright centre was

For Series III models, new style of combined hub cap and trim became standard, finish varying according to model. These examples are from a 4.2 Daimler Sovereign (above, with 'D' on centre cap and matt black centre section) and a Jaguar V12 model (above right, with 'leaper' on centre cap and unpainted centre section).

Further adaptation of Series III combined wheel trim came with 'separation' of the Daimler marque in the early '80s – Daimlers acquired an elaborate stainless steel hub cap.

contained within the black section, and 5.3-litre models had all brightwork with no black.

This type of wheel trim was specified for all models including the Vanden Plas saloons. The Daimler Double-Six retained the ventilated chromed wheels with chrome hub caps.

From 1981 the tyre section on V12-engined saloons was increased from 205mm to 215mm and remained the same throughout the remainder of production. At the same time new Pirelli P5 tyres were offered on Jaguar saloons.

From April 1982 a new type of GKN alloy

From Series II V12s to very last Daimler Double-Sixes, Kent alloy wheels (right) were standard for various models and an extra-cost option for others. Tread pattern (far right) on the original Dunlop tyres designed for the XJ6.

The 'pepperpot' alloy wheel was introduced for the Jaguar Series III mid-term, used as standard on Jaguar Sovereign models throughout production.

perforated wheel (later known as 'pepperpot') was introduced in bright silver finish carrying two concentric circles of 20 holes. Still with exposed wheel nuts and centre cap with Jaguar 'growler' in silver, initially these were offered only on the Jaguar V12 HE model. With the introduction of the Jaguar Sovereign range for the 1984 model year, they became standard on both six-cylinder and V12 cars and continued in use right to the end of V12 production in 1992, even being requested to special order by some Daimler customers.

For 1983 there were more wheel trim changes with the introduction of a new stainless steel trim and highly polished hub cap arrangement for the six-cylinder Daimler models (including the VDP version). As before the trim was held on by the wheel nuts but the new flush-fitting bright hub cap snapped into position over the wheel nuts, resulting in a very smooth and uncluttered look. As usual a 'D' script was incorporated in a centre cap arrangement with a black background. This type of trim arrangement only lasted until the introduction of the Jaguar Sovereign models and the rationalisation of Daimlers. During this Daimler 'hub cap' period, the Double-Six and Vanden Plas versions used either this type as standard or the GKN Kent alloy wheel. The Kent alloy became a standard feature thereafter on Daimler models right up to the end of production in 1992.

No Series I, II or III models were ever offered with wire-spoked wheels and owners were strongly discouraged from fitting such wheels.

Optional Equipment & Accessories

All Jaguar XJ saloons were well equipped from new, although, as already covered elsewhere, the 2.8-litre 'Standard' model (which was listed although doubtfully produced) did not feature some of the more luxurious items of the other models. These, however, could have been specified to match the higher-priced cars if ordered at the time of purchase. This was the situation throughout the life of the XJ Series as many owners chose to equip their new cars with all manner of extra-cost items to suit their individual requirements. This makes it very difficult to arrive at definitive specification for each model.

It is not practical here to identify many of the after-market accessories that could have been purchased through non-Jaguar sources during the heyday of the XJs. Many items such as spot and fog lamps, over-mats, sound systems, etc, were just as suitable for a Jaguar as any other car. Instead we will look at extra-cost options that an owner could have specified from the factory when ordering an XJ saloon. This will inevitably include many items that were standard on selected models at some time during production, so cross-reference will be needed with the relevant chapters elsewhere in this book.

Electrically-heated rear window
This was standard on all cars over the years except for the 2.8-litre cars, 4.2-litre Jaguars and Daimlers until 1972, and all 3.4-litre cars until 1982.

Overdrive
Overdrive was naturally only ever available on the manual transmission cars and was standard equipment on all models except for the 2.8-litre 'Standard' version. With the introduction of the five-speed manual gearbox on Series III models, the fifth gear acted as an overdrive equivalent so no separate overdrive unit was available.

Transmissions
Automatic transmission was a quoted option for Series I/II and early Series III six-cylinder cars, but always standard for the V12 models, which were never offered with a manual alternative. Automatic became the norm on all Series III cars after the demise of the five-speed gearbox in the 1981 model year. For the various types of transmission used, refer to the *Transmission* chapter (page 100).

Power-assisted steering
This came on all models except for the 2.8-litre 'Standard' saloon, on which it was an extra-cost option. Police Specification saloons were never equipped with power-assisted steering either.

Electrically-operated windows
These were an extra-cost option on all models until 1974 except for the Vanden Plas Double-Six Series I, on which they were standard. After 1974 electric windows were an extra-cost option on 3.4-litre Series II models only. On all others they became standard equipment and the norm. Again Police Specification XJ saloons of all types were never equipped with electric windows.

Fog/spot lamps & headlamps
Auxiliary lighting was of two specific types, both supplied by Lucas. Firstly, there were the back-mounted rectangular lamps fitted to replace the existing dummy horn grilles on the Series I cars. These were an extra-cost option on all models except the Vanden Plas Double-Six, on which they were standard. They could have been fitted to any Series I models.

Secondly, the later under-bumper rectangular lamps were an extra-cost option on all Series II and III models except for the Vanden Plas versions, on which they were standard. The style changed slightly, becoming larger and with protective black covers for Series III models. This type became standard on all Daimler models post-1983 but remained an extra for Jaguars at all times.

As far as headlamps were concerned, from 1976 halogen units became an extra-cost option for all Jaguar and Daimler models but by 1979 were standard on all Series III cars except the 3.4-litre base models.

Air conditioning
Air conditioning was never available as an option on the 2.8-litre saloons. It was an extra-cost option on all other Series I models except for the

Fog lamp fitting on Series I models (right), replacing the existing horn grilles, and on Series IIs (far right).

Early type of Kangol inertia reel seat belt mechanism (right) fitted to many Series I models. Later Kangol style (far right) adopted from the introduction of the Vanden Plas model.

Some early XJ6s were originally fitted with seat belts carrying the BMC logo (right), but most featured the Jaguar 'leaper' in the form shown (far right). On the seat back is the black plastic clip to hold the buckle.

Double-Six Vanden Plas, which was the first ever model from Jaguar to have it fitted as standard. Air conditioning remained an extra-cost option on Series II models (except for the Vanden Plas six-cylinder and V12 models) until 1974, when it became standard on the V12 Series II Daimlers and Coupés – until British Leyland reduced the specification and made it an extra again. It is recorded that 20 V12 Coupés left the factory without air conditioning.

From October 1983 air conditioning became a standard feature on all Daimlers plus Jaguar Sovereigns. On less expensive Jaguar models the normal heating system remained standard.

Seat belts

Three types of seat belt were available over the life of the Series XJs: a simple lap and diagonal or inertia reel or, for the rear compartment, single diagonal. Front belts were an extra-cost option on all models until 1972, coloured black or charcoal according to production batch. At that time they became standard on the Vanden Plas Series I.

Because these early belts were not of the inertia reel type, the loose buckles could be stored in a black plastic clip fastened to the inner seat back side panel. The buckles themselves were finished in crackle black plastic with a glued-on label showing the Daimler or Jaguar name with 'D' script or 'leaper' as appropriate in black on silver, or the BMC name with 'rosette' logo.

By 1973 all models had front seat belts fitted as standard. Similarly rear belts only became standard on VDP cars from 1975 and remained an extra-cost option for 3.4-litre and 4.2-litre models (except Daimlers) until the introduction of Jaguar Sovereign models, when rear belts were standardised on all cars.

Laminated windscreen

Initially only an extra-cost option on all models except the Vanden Plas Double-Six Series I, from 1974 a laminated windscreen became standard on Series II models and on all subsequent models.

Tinted/Sundym glass

This was an extra-cost item on all Jaguar and Daimler models until the introduction of the Vanden Plas Series I saloon, on which it became standard equipment and subsequently for all V12 cars from 1976. From 1978 all models except the 3.4-litre gained tinted glass as standard. Prior to this it could be requested for any model.

Radio/tape systems

These were all extra-cost items initially, and for the first couple of years Jaguar left the installation of equipment to individual choice, not listing any approved sets. Dealers usually recommended contemporary Radiomobile or Philips equipment.

From 1971 the listed extra-cost equipment included the then unique Philips four-speaker radio with a stereo cassette tape recorder (which itself was a rarity as most luxury car manufacturers were specifying cartridge players at this time). The system also came complete with a rear-mounted electric aerial. Alternatively a cheaper option listed was the Radiomobile 1085T two-speaker system without electric aerial.

From 1972 the Philips system was deleted in favour of the Radiomobile 108SR, incorporating a cartridge player. This system, with four speakers, became standard on the Series I Vanden Plas but was usually only fitted with two speakers on other

models. A Phillips RN712 four-speaker radio with stereo cassette player became listed as an extra-cost item for all models at this time, but here again could well have been fitted to some cars with only two front-mounted speakers.

Vanden Plas Series I models were also available with a special conversion of the Philips four-speaker radio/tape player incorporating a recording system. A black-crackle finished socket and microphone holder were bolted to the underside of the passenger-side dashboard and a separate microphone with on/off switch and DIN plug connector was used to activate the tape.

By 1974 the budget Radiomobile 1085T system also became available with four speakers and an electric aerial if requested. It was upgraded in 1975 to the 1085S and by 1976 this was fitted

Highly specialised dictation equipment was an optional extra on Series I models. It used an integrated microphone system to the cassette deck built into the radio unit.

Parcel shelf position of the rear compartment speaker when a radio was fitted to earlier cars without door speakers – this was normally on the driver's side of the shelf.

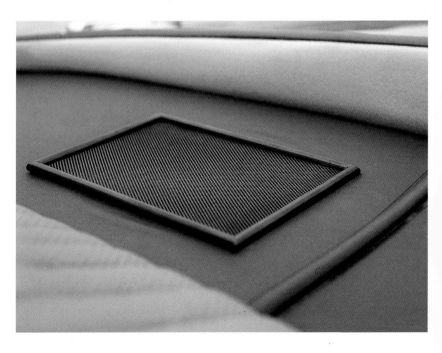

the Philips AC420 unit due to shortage of supply.

In September 1983 the Philips systems were completely replaced by more sophisticated Clarion electronic stereo radio/cassette systems. The PU7009A system was adopted as standard on Daimler and Jaguar Sovereign models and was available at extra cost on other cars. A higher-powered PU9021A system was used on the very last of the Vanden Plas models and for the top-of-the-range export-specification cars.

More changes came in November 1984 with the use on all cars of the Clarion E950 hi-fi stereo radio/cassette system with dual intensity lighting. It was standard on Sovereigns and Daimlers and remained in use virtually until the end of production. However, in 1991 Jaguar announced the availability of a brand new integrated radio/stereo tape player also adaptable for a CD autochanger, the latter an extra-cost option installed either at the factory or by dealers. This later unit is easily

Initial position on Series I cars for the manual radio aerial was on the front wing (above). Later Series I and all Series II models had the aerial on the rear wing (right), on either left or right according to period. All Series III aerials were of much better quality, this example (far right) showing the Merlin style fitted to a late-model XJ6.

from new as standard equipment on the Daimler Double-Six two-door.

For the 1976 model year Jaguar also started to fit radios as standard equipment on other models, namely the Radiomobile 1085S to Jaguar and Daimler V12 cars (saloons and Coupés), although you still had to pay extra for the two rear speakers and an electric aerial. The 108SR radio/cartridge system also remained an extra and a new Philips system was introduced, the RN642 radio/cassette complete with four speakers and electric aerial.

Great strides forward were made for 1978 and the launch of the Series III models as all cars came fitted as standard with a new Philips AC460 mono radio/stereo cassette plus electric aerial and four speakers. Alternatively and at extra cost (except for the Vanden Plas model where it was standard) was the Philips AC860 premier system. From 1980 a Philips GCA637 radio/cassette system was also available but this was superseded in 1983 by

identifiable by the 'flipper' control to seek radio stations, tape movement and CD track selection. The new unit also incorporated anti-theft coding and a flashing LED warning light.

Where the CD player was specified, this was situated in the boot below the rear window shelf and next to the relocated battery. The electrical harness was pre-fitted to all cars at the factory regardless of audio equipment.

It should be borne in mind that a customer could have specified the installation of any other equipment to individual requirement, or indeed asked the dealer to change the system supplied by Jaguar. Therefore it should not necessarily be considered incorrect to find alternative systems in Series Jaguars today if they are fitted correctly.

Early Series Is used a pull-up aerial mounted towards the rear of the front wing or on the rear wing, both on the driver's side. An electric aerial became standard on Vanden Plas models from their introduction in 1972 and an extra-cost option on all others. Most of these aerials were made by Merlin but, due to unreliability, were replaced in 1981 by a Radiomobile-manufactured version. Some owners preferred manual roof-mounted aerials fitted above the windscreen, but usually these are only found on Series I cars.

Wheels

The chrome-plated snap-on rimbellishers featured on Series I 4.2-litre cars were an extra-cost option on 2.8-litre models. From the launch of the Vanden Plas in 1972, chrome-plated equivalents to the steel ventilated wheels were offered. As used previously on the E-type Series III, these would still take the hub caps but without the need for rimbellishers. At that time these were still extra-cost options on all models including VDPs and remained available until 1977.

By the end of 1975 a new style of alloy wheel called the Kent (produced by GKN) became available specifically for the V12 saloons and Coupés. It was of the same type used on the XJ-S and was an extra-cost option only. These Kent alloys became standard from 1984, when they were standardised on Daimlers unless the Jaguar-style 'pepperpots' were specified (see below).

With the introduction of the Jaguar Sovereign models from October 1983 these top-of-the-range Jaguar models featured the then new 'pepperpot' alloys, which became an alternative no-cost option on Daimlers from 1984. The 'pepperpots' were also listed as an extra-cost option on all other XJ models at this time and remained so until the end of production.

Conventional XJ6 3.4-litre and 4.2-litre Series III models were never equipped as standard with alloy wheels, using instead the stainless steel spring-loaded shaped hub cap arrangement.

Tyres

Whitewall tyres were always an extra-cost option on all models not destined for the US market. For US markets a thin wall or continuous heavy white band could be specified.

Exterior mirrors

Conventional chrome-plated wing mirrors in a notchback style were available as an extra-cost option on Series I cars; export models featured a door-mounted variety as standard from mid-term production. This later type was also offered throughout the production of low-specification Series II models.

A remotely-adjustable (non-electric) door mirror became available first on the Series I Vanden Plas model; only the driver's side mirror was standard but a passenger side mirror could be ordered at extra cost. From 1975 the driver's side mirror was an extra-cost option on all other cars. These mirrors were of the same type and style as used on the early XJ-S models.

Remote-control mirrors were always fitted to the Series III models (see *Body Trim*, page 34), with electric operation standard on Sovereigns and Daimlers but otherwise an extra-cost option.

Head restraints

Until August 1969 front seat head restraints were not available. From then on they were an extra-cost item on Series I cars for the front seats only and in the perforated leather style. Purchasers of a Daimler Series I (without perforated upholstery) still got the perforated style of head restraint. Series I Vanden Plas models had front seat head restraints in smooth leather as standard.

Front head restraints became standard on all Series II cars, except for the 3.4-litre models and the few 2.8-litre cars produced at that time. At this time restraints for the rear seat passengers were only fitted to VDP models. When rear head restraints became standard on Sovereign and Daimler models in 1983, they also became available as extra-cost items for the other models.

Mud flaps

These became available as accessories for new cars from 1972. All featured Jaguar or Daimler script until well into the Series III models. From 1988 a new style was used without a name.

Cruise control

This was only ever listed as an extra-cost option for the Series III models and initially was available only for the 4.2- and 5.3-litre cars. Cruise control became standard on 5.3-litre Sovereign and Daimler models in 1983.

Electric front seat tilt adjustment

This was available from June 1979 on Series III models as an extra-cost option for the driver's seat only. It then became standard on Sovereign and Daimler models from 1983 (for both driver and front seat passenger) and was available thereafter on other models at extra cost.

Sliding sunroof/wind deflector

This was never listed as a Jaguar extra-cost option for Series I and II models. A couple of outside companies produced a manually-operated metal sunroof, which was expertly fitted as an after-market accessory on Series IIs for many dealers.

An electric metal integrated sunroof panel was listed as an extra-cost option for any model from the introduction of the Series III, but had to be specified when ordering a car as two distinct bodyshells were produced, one with and the other without the sunroof fittings. The sunroof was only

Example of the contemporary manually adjustable door mirror specified by Jaguar.

Electric sunroof became available for Series III, but was standard only on the Daimler Double-Six from 1986.

ever fitted as standard on the Daimler Double-Six from 1986, although many other models did have one, either by customer request or through dealers placing 'stock' orders.

A tinted acrylic wind deflector was introduced in 1986. It could be ordered with a sunroof and was permanently attached to the outside of the roof on the leading edge of the opening.

Roof accessories

Jaguar even offered a roof rack for the Series III saloons from 1985. The two-bar carrier arrangement was lockable and finished in matt black. It was available with a choice of specialised fittings including luggage frame, roof box in GRP (two-tone grey finish), luggage net, cycle holder, ski holder, sailboard holder or mountain bike holder.

Headlamp wash/wipe

Listed as an extra-cost option on all Series III models, this was only standardised on the VDP from 1979, then on the Jaguar Sovereign V12 from October 1983, and on Daimlers from 1985.

Limited-slip differential

Only listed as an extra-cost option from the introduction of the Series II models and then standardised on all V12-engined cars.

Trip computer

Only ever available on Series III models, from the introduction of the Jaguar Sovereign in October

1983. It was standard on these cars and subsequent Daimlers but optional on others. It was possible to order a new Daimler or Sovereign without the computer, in which case it was replaced by the rectangular analogue clock from the lesser models.

Carpets/mats/rugs/upholstery

Black leather interior trim was always an extra-cost item on all XJ Series saloons.

Leather upholstery was always an extra-cost option on 3.4-litre models. Models that normally had leather upholstery could be trimmed with cloth to special order at no extra cost.

The rubber interior floor mats were rectangular and not shaped to the footwells for Series I and II ranges, but they did carry the 'D' script or Jaguar 'leaper'. With the introduction of Series III cars, shaped mats with script were available, the style amended from the 1984 model year to a pre-formed plastic that was harder and shinier.

Tailored over-carpets with a driver's heel pad were also available for Series III models from 1985 in the form of a tufted weave shaped to fit loosely over the existing carpets. Colours were slate, rattan, smoke, winebury, champagne or sage.

Passenger footwell rugs were only ever standard on Vanden Plas and Daimler Double-Six cars, in lambswool on Series I models but nylon on all later cars. Colours were beige, champagne, tan, slate or doeskin. From 1990 sheepskin over-rugs of a slightly different shape were available, to suit changes to the interior trim on the later cars. Colours were slate or champagne.

Door edge guards

Made from plastic-coated flexible light alloy, these were available to fit all four doors on the Series III XJ models from around 1988 until the end of production.

Wooden gear knob

A walnut-finished gear knob could be ordered for the automatic transmission quadrant and was a simple screw fit (in two sections) to replace the existing black plastic type. It was available for Series III installation from 1986 onwards.

Tow bar

Contemporary tow bars were available from renowned companies like Witter for all of these Jaguars, but with the Series III models Jaguar introduced its own version, which included all fittings and wiring connections.

Telephones

Jaguar offered a mobile telephone installation from the 1988 model year for the Series III saloons. Siting of the handset was in the centre console armrest, as on contemporary XJ40 models.

Data Section

IDENTIFICATION

Marque	Model	Made From	Made To	First Chassis/VIN Number RHD	LHD	Transmission/Market
	Series I					
Jaguar	XJ6 2.8 Litre	Sep 1968	May 1973	1G.1001	1G.50001	All
Daimler	Sovereign 2.8 Litre	Oct 1969	May 1973	1T.1001	N/A	All
Jaguar	XJ6 4.2 Litre	Sep 1968	Jul 1973	1L.1001	1L.50001	All
Daimler	Sovereign 4.2 Litre	Oct 1969	Jul 1973	1U.1001	N/A	All
Jaguar	XJ6 4.2 Long Wheelbase	Oct 1972	Jul 1973	2E.1001	2E.50001	All
Daimler	Sovereign 4.2 LWB	Oct 1972	Jul 1973	2D.1001	N/A	All
Jaguar	XJ12 5.3 Litre V12	Jul 1972	Aug 1973	1P.1001	1P.50001	All
Daimler	Double-Six	Jul 1972	Aug 1973	2A.1001	2A.50001	All
Jaguar	XJ12L Long Wheelbase	Oct 1972	Aug 1973	2C.1001	2C.50001	All
Daimler	Double-Six Vanden Plas	Sep 1972	Aug 1973	2B.1001	2B.50001	All
	Series II					
Jaguar	XJ6 2.8 Litre	Sep 1973	Nov 1973	N/A	2U.50001	All
Jaguar	XJ6 4.2 Litre	Sep 1973	Nov 1974	2N.1001	2N.50001	All
Daimler	Sovereign 4.2 Litre	Sep 1973	Nov 1974	2M.1001	2M.50001	All
Jaguar	XJ6L 4.2 Long Wheelbase	Sep 1973	Feb 1979	2T.1001	2T.50001	All
Daimler	Sovereign 4.2 LWB	Sep 1973	Feb 1979	2S.1001	2S.50001	All
Jaguar	XJ12L Long Wheelbase	Sep 1973	Feb 1979	2R.1001	2R.50001	All
Daimler	Double-Six LWB	Sep 1973	Feb 1979	2K.1001	2K.50001	All
Daimler	Double-Six Vanden Plas	Sep 1973	Feb 1979	2P.1001	2P.50001	All
Jaguar	XJ6C 4.2 Litre Coupé	Oct 1974*	Nov 1977	2J.1001	2J.50001	All
Daimler	Sovereign 4.2 Two-door	Oct 1974*	Nov 1977	2H.1001	2H.50001	All
Jaguar	XJ12C 5.3 V12 Coupé	Oct 1974*	Nov 1977	2G.1001	2G.50001	All
Daimler	Double-Six Two-door	Oct 1974*	Nov 1977	2F.1001	2F.50001	All
Jaguar	XJ 3.4 Litre	Apr 1975	Feb 1979	3A.1001	3A.50001	All
Daimler	Sovereign 3.4 Litre	Apr 1975	Feb 1979	3B.1001	3B.50001	All
Daimler	Vanden Plas 4.2 Litre	Apr 1975	Feb 1979	3C.1001	3C.50001	All
	Series III					
Jaguar	XJ6 3.4 Litre	Mar 1979	Apr 1987	JAAL.A.3CC	JAAL.A.4CC	Auto UK
Jaguar	XJ6 3.4 Litre	Mar 1979	Apr 1987	JAAL.A.7CC	JAAL.A.8CC	Manual UK
Daimler	XJ6 3.4 Litre	Mar 1979	Oct 1982	DCAL.A.3CC	DCAL.A.4CC	Auto UK
Daimler	XJ6 3.4 Litre	Mar 1979	Oct 1982	DCAL.A.7CC	DCAL.A.8CC	Manual UK
Jaguar	XJ6 4.2 Litre	Mar 1979	Apr 1987	JAAL.P.3CC	JAAL.P.4CC	Auto UK
Jaguar	XJ6 4.2 Litre	Mar 1979	Apr 1987	JAAL.P.7CC	JAAL.P.8CC	Manual UK
Daimler	Sovereign 4.2 Litre	Mar 1979	Jul 1986	DCAL.P.3CC	DCAL.P.4CC	Auto UK
Daimler	Sovereign 4.2 Litre	Mar 1979	Jul 1986	DCAL.P.7CC	DCAL.P.8CC	Manual UK
Jaguar	XJ6 4.2 Litre	Mar 1979	Apr 1987	N/A	JAVL.N.49C	Auto Canada/US
Jaguar	XJ6 4.2 Litre	Mar 1979	Apr 1987	JAAL.R.3CC	N/A	Auto Australia
Jaguar	XJ6 4.2 Litre	Mar 1979	Apr 1987	N/A	JAAL.R.4CC	Auto Sweden
Jaguar	XJ6 4.2 Litre	Mar 1979	Apr 1987	JAJL.N.3CC	JAJL.N.4CC	Auto Japan
Daimler	Sovereign 4.2 Litre	Mar 1979	Jul 1986	DCAL.R.3CC	N/A	Auto Australia
Daimler	Vanden Plas 4.2 Litre	Mar 1979	Oct 1982	DCRL.P.3CC	DCRL.P.4CC	UK
Daimler	Vanden Plas 4.2 Litre	Mar 1979	Oct 1982	DCAL.R.3CC	N/A	Australia
Jaguar	XJ12 5.3 Litre V12	Mar 1979	Nov 1991	JBAL.W.3CC	JBAL.W.4CC	UK
Jaguar	XJ12 5.3 Litre V12	Mar 1979	Nov 1991	N/A	JBVL.V.49C	US/Canada
Jaguar	XJ12 5.3 Litre V12	Mar 1979	Nov 1991	JBAL.Y.3CC	N/A	Australia
Jaguar	XJ12 5.3 Litre V12	Mar 1979	Nov 1991	JBJL.V.3CC	JBJL.V.4CC	Japan
Jaguar	XJ12 5.3 Litre V12	Jun 1983	Nov 1991	N/A	JBVL.X.49C	California only
Daimler	Double-Six Vanden Plas	Mar 1979	Oct 1982	DDRL.W.3CC	DDRL.W.4CC	UK
Daimler	Double-Six Vanden Plas	Mar 1979	Oct 1982	DDRL.Y.3CC	N/A	Australia
Daimler	Double-Six Vanden Plas	Mar 1979	Oct 1982	DDRL.V.3CC	N/A	Japan
Daimler	Double-Six	Mar 1979	Nov 1992	DDAL.W.3CC	DDAL.W.4CC	UK
Daimler	Double-Six	Mar 1979	Nov 1992	DDAL.Y.3CC	N/A	Australia

* Announced in Sep 1973 but not in production until Oct 1974.

Earlier and later styles of windscreen sticker, although in some cases Series I 2.8-litre models received the sticker normally found on earlier 240 models!

PRODUCTION FIGURES

XJ SERIES I

Marque	Model	Wheelbase	Number
Jaguar	XJ6 2.8 Litre	Short	19,322
Daimler	Sovereign 2.8 Litre	Short	3233
Jaguar	XJ6 4.2 Litre	Short	59,077
Daimler	Sovereign 4.2 Litre	Short	11,522
Jaguar	XJ6L 4.2 Litre	Long	874
Daimler	Sovereign 4.2 Litre	Long	386
Jaguar	XJ12 5.3 Litre	Short	2474
Daimler	Double-Six	Short	534
Jaguar	XJ12L 5.3 litre	Long	754
Daimler	Double-Six Vanden Plas	Long	351
Total Series I Production			**98,527**

XJ SERIES II

Marque	Model	Wheelbase	Number
Jaguar	XJ6 2.8 Litre	Short	170
Jaguar	XJ 3.4 Litre	Short	6880
Daimler	Sovereign 3.4 Litre	Short	2341
Jaguar	XJ6 4.2 Litre	Short	12,147
Daimler	Sovereign 4.2 Litre	Short	2435
Jaguar	XJ6L 4.2 Litre	Long	57,804
Daimler	Sovereign & Vanden Plas 4.2 Litre	Long	14,531
Jaguar	XJ4.2C Coupé	Short	6487
Daimler	Sovereign Two-door 4.2 Litre	Short	1677
Jaguar	XJ12L 5.3 Litre	Long	16,010
Daimler	Double-Six	Long	2608
Jaguar	XJ5.3C Coupé	Short	1855
Daimler	Double-Six Two-door	Short	407
Daimler	Double-Six Vanden Plas	Long	1726
Total Series II Production			**127,078**

XJ SERIES III

Marque	Model	Wheelbase	Number
Jaguar	XJ6 3.4 Litre	Long	5799
Jaguar	XJ6 4.2 Litre	Long	97,349
Jaguar	Sovereign 4.2 Litre	Long	27,261
Daimler	Sovereign 4.2 Litre	Long	20,315
Daimler	Vanden Plas 4.2 Litre	Long	1953
Jaguar	XJ12 5.3 Litre	Long	5408
Jaguar	Sovereign 5.3 Litre	Long	9129
Daimler	Double-Six	Long	9628
Daimler	Double-Six Vanden Plas	Long	401
Total Series III Production			**177,243**
Total XJ Series Production			**402,848**

Early style of battery earthing legend (right), later moved to the battery carrier or rear of engine bulkhead area in the form of a label. Most Series II and later models carried a more specific warning label (below) behind the battery itself as the electronics became more sophisticated.

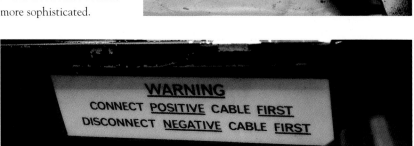

JAGUAR & DAIMLER SERIES I 4.2 LITRE COLOUR SCHEMES (SEP 1968 TO OCT 1972)

Because of changing paint technology there is no longer a need to identify the specific types of paint finishes used on Jaguar XJ models. The range of paint colours varied considerably throughout production and again it must be pointed out that at times owners could and did specify individual requirements either from or outside the existing Jaguar range. These cannot be accounted for here but some sort of record should still be available to individual owners by contacting the Jaguar Daimler Heritage Trust with the appropriate VIN number. This should reveal any special features on a particular model.

Paint	Trim
Old English White	Red
	Light Blue
	Dark Blue
Warwick Grey	Red
	Dark Blue
	Cinnamon
Ascot Fawn	Red
	Cinnamon
	Beige
Willow Green	Suede Green
	Beige
	Grey
	Cinnamon
Dark Blue	Red
	Light Blue
	Grey
Sable Brown	Grey
	Beige
	Cinnamon
Light Blue	Dark Blue
	Grey
	Light Blue
British Racing Green	Suede Green
	Beige
	Cinnamon
Regency Red	Grey
	Beige
Black	Red
	Grey
	Cinnamon
Signal Red*	Black
	Beige
Pale Primrose*	Red
	Beige
	Black
Azure Blue*	Dark Blue
	Beige
	Cinnamon
Light Silver*	Red
	Beige
	Black
	Dark Blue

Note * These colours were always an extra-cost addition to the XJ saloon colour range.

Special seat belt anchorage information legend within the engine bay on Series I models.

JAGUAR & DAIMLER SERIES I 2.8 LITRE COLOUR SCHEMES (SEP 1968 TO OCT 1972)

Any of the standard range of XJ 4.2 paint colours could be specified. Choice of interior trim, in Ambla only, was restricted to Red, Beige, Dark Blue or Black.

JAGUAR & DAIMLER SERIES I & II 2.8, 3.4, 4.2 & 5.3 LITRE COLOUR SCHEMES (OCT 1972 TO OCT 1974)

Paint	Trim
Old English White	Red
	French Blue (mid to dark)
	Dark Blue
Fern Grey (green)	Moss Green
	Olive
	Tan
Regency Red	Biscuit
	Cinnamon
	Red
Turquoise	Tan
	Terracotta
	Cinnamon
Dark Blue	Red
	French Blue
	Biscuit
Greensand (dark beige)	Tan
	Olive
	Cinnamon
Sable Brown	Biscuit
	Moss Green
	Cinnamon
Heather (dark pink)	Maroon
	Antelope
	Cerise
British Racing Green	Moss Green
	Biscuit
	Cinnamon
Lavender (pale purple)	French Blue
	Biscuit
	Dark Blue

Notes The same combination of extra-cost colours applied as in the 1968-72 list. Remaining 2.8-litre models that fell within this time scale also had this revised colour range

DAIMLER VANDEN PLAS SERIES I/II SPECIALIST COLOUR SCHEMES

Paint	Trim
Silver Sand (pale gold)	Chamois (mid beige)
	Tuscan (mid tan)
	Deep Olive
Caramel (deep gold)	Chamois
	Tuscan
	Deep Olive
Coral	Chamois
	Tuscan
	Deep Olive
Aegean Blue (mid to dark blue)	Chamois
	Tuscan
	Deep Olive
Sage	Chamois
	Tuscan
	Deep Olive
Morello (dark cherry red)	Chamois
	Tuscan
	Deep Olive
Aubergine	Chamois
	Tuscan
	Deep Olive

Notes Colours only for the Vanden Plas Series I Double-Six models. Any exterior colour scheme could be ordered with one of the three interior trim colours. All vinyl roof coverings were in black and wheels were painted silver. Vanden Plas colours remained constant throughout Series I and II production until 1977, when Aegean Blue was changed to the lighter colour of Biascan Blue.

JAGUAR & DAIMLER SERIES II COLOUR SCHEMES (OCT 1974 TO SEP 1975)

Paint	Trim
Old English White	Russet
	Dark Blue
	Cinnamon
Fern Grey	Moss Green
	Olive
	Cinnamon
Greensand	Olive
	Biscuit
	Cinnamon
Sable Brown	Biscuit
	Moss Green
	Cinnamon
Regency Red	Biscuit
	Cinnamon
	Russet
British Racing Green	Moss Green
	Biscuit
	Cinnamon
Lavender Blue	Cinnamon
	Biscuit
	Dark Blue
Dark Blue	Russet
	Dark Blue
	Biscuit

Notes During the above period Black was not a standard interior trim colour but could be specified either in leather or cloth (Ebony) with any of the exterior paint finishes. Silver, Primrose, Black and Signal Red were special order exterior paint finishes on Series II XJ models. Cloth interior trim colours, available in any combination to match exterior finishes, were: Navy, Garnet, Fawn and Sand.

Earliest style of chassis plate (top) on nearside front inner wing, and early Series I V12 plate (above) on offside inner wing near the radiator.

Series II Jaguar and Daimler chassis plates, from slightly different periods. Both show British Leyland parentage.

Examples of earlier (British Leyland) and later under-bonnet stickers for engine information.

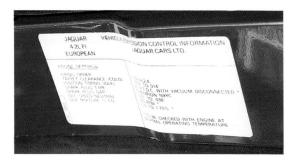

JAGUAR & DAIMLER SERIES II SALOON/COUPÉ COLOUR SCHEMES
(OCTOBER 1975 TO END OF SERIES II PRODUCTION)

Paint	Trim Material	Trim Colour
Old English White	Leather	Russet
	Leather	Cinnamon
	Cloth	Sand
	Cloth	Garnet
Juniper Green (mid)	Leather	Biscuit
	Leather	Cinnamon
	Cloth	Sand
Carriage Brown (dark)	Leather	Biscuit
	Leather	Cinnamon
	Cloth	Sand
Moroccan Bronze	Leather	Biscuit
	Leather	Cinnamon
	Cloth	Sand
Regency Red	Leather	Biscuit
	Leather	Cinnamon
	Cloth	Sand
British Racing Green	Leather	Biscuit
	Leather	Cinnamon
	Cloth	Sand
Squadron Blue (mid)	Leather	Dark Blue
	Leather	Biscuit
	Cloth	Sand
	Cloth	Navy
Dark Blue	Leather	Biscuit
	Leather	Russet
	Cloth	Sand
	Cloth	Garnet

Notes Extra-cost paint finishes remained as before: Black, Signal Red, Primrose and Silver. Interior trim in Black (leather) or Ebony (cloth) also remained an extra-cost option on all models.

JAGUAR & DAIMLER SERIES III COLOUR SCHEMES (1979-80)

Paint	Trim Material	Trim Colour
Tudor White	Leather	Russet
	Leather	Biscuit
	Cloth	Garnet
	Cloth	Sand
Cotswold Yellow	Leather	Cinnamon
	Leather	Dark Blue
	Cloth	Sand
	Cloth	Navy
Damson Red	Leather	Russet
	Leather	Cinnamon
	Cloth	Garnet
	Cloth	Sand
Racing Green Metallic	Leather	Biscuit
	Leather	Cinnamon
	Cloth	Sand
Silver Frost Metallic	Leather	Russet
	Leather	Dark Blue
	Cloth	Garnet
	Cloth	Sand
Cobalt Blue Metallic	Leather	Cinnamon
	Leather	Dark Blue
	Cloth	Sand
	Cloth	Navy
Quartz Blue Metallic (light)	Leather	Biscuit
	Leather	Dark Blue
	Cloth	Sand
	Cloth	Navy
Chestnut Brown Metallic	Leather	Cinnamon
	Leather	Biscuit
	Cloth	Sand
Sebring Red*	Leather	Biscuit
	Leather	Dark Blue
	Cloth	Sand
	Cloth	Navy
Black*	Leather	Biscuit
	Leather	Russet
	Cloth	Garnet
	Cloth	Sand

Notes * Still extra-cost alternative colour schemes. Other extra-cost alternatives for interior leather colour schemes included Chamois, Deep Olive, Blue-Grey, Tan or Maroon. The range was standardised for all models, including base 3.4-litre saloons, at this time.

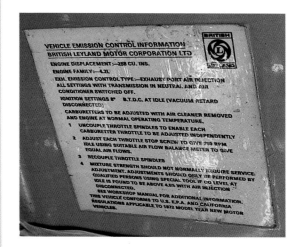

Under-bonnet US federal emissions control information required by law on Series I models.

DAIMLER VANDEN PLAS SERIES III 4.2 & 5.3 LITRE COLOUR SCHEMES
(1979 TO END OF PRODUCTION IN 1983)

Paint	Interior Trim
Silver Sand	Chamois
	Olive
	Tan
Caramel	Chamois
	Olive
	Tan
Coral	Chamois
	Olive
	Tan
Biascan Blue	Chamois
	Olive
	Tan
Mistletoe (light gold)	Chamois
	Olive
	Tan
Mink (brown)	Chamois
	Olive
	Tan
Amethyst	Chamois
	Olive
	Tan

JAGUAR & DAIMLER SERIES III COLOUR SCHEMES, ALL MODELS (1984/1985 MODEL YEARS)

Paint
Tudor White
Black
Clarendon Blue (dark)
Grosvenor Brown (dark)
Cirrus Grey
Cranberry Metallic
Rhodium Silver Metallic
Cobalt Blue Metallic
Sapphire Blue Metallic (light)
Racing Green Metallic
Antelope Metallic (light gold)
Coronet Gold Metallic (bright)*
Sage Green Metallic
Regent Grey Metallic (dark)
Claret Metallic
Silversand Metallic

Notes Leather or cloth interior colours were available at customer choice to combine with any of the exterior paint colours, as follows. Leather: Biscuit, Black, Buckskin, Doeskin, Isis Blue, Mulberry or Savile Grey. Cloth: Beige, Fleet Blue (dark), Graphite or Parchment (added as a further cloth upholstery option for 1985 model year).
* Coronet Gold paint was deleted for the 1985 model year.

Earlier Series III style of chassis plate, still sited on the inner wing.

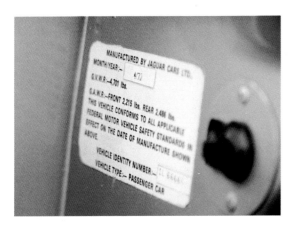

Evolution of A-post vehicle identification stickers.

JAGUAR & DAIMLER SERIES III COLOUR SCHEMES, ALL MODELS (1981-83)

Paint
Tudor White
Black
Indigo Blue
Grosvenor Brown (dark)
Portland Beige
Sebring Red
Rhodium Silver Metallic
Cobalt Blue Metallic
Sapphire Blue Metallic (light)
Racing Green Metallic
Chestnut Metallic
Coronet Gold Metallic (bright)
Sable Brown Metallic
Claret Metallic
Silversand Metallic

Notes Leather or cloth interior colours were available at customer choice to combine with any of the exterior paint colours, as follows. Leather: Biscuit, County Tan, Isis Blue, Black, Doeskin or Burnt Umber. Cloth: Beige, Amber, Fleet Blue (dark) or Graphite.

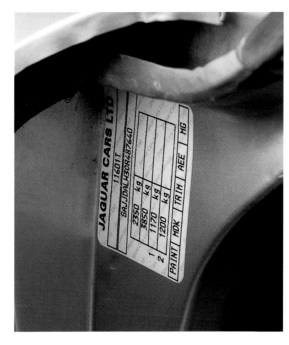

Jaguar & Daimler Series III Colour Schemes, All Models (1986 model year)

Paint
Black
Tudor White
Windsor Blue (dark)
Sebring Red
Jaguar Racing Green
Cirrus Grey
Steel Metallic (Mid grey/blue)
Cobalt Blue Metallic
Regent Grey Metallic (dark)
Rhodium Silver Metallic
Antelope Metallic
Silversand Metallic
Claret Metallic
Cranberry Metallic
Curlew Brown Metallic
Sage Green Metallic

Notes At this point Jaguar expanded its interim trim range and replaced the cloth upholstery with a new wool tweed style. The company also issued a preferred list of matches of trim to body colour but owners could still specify any combination within the offered range, as follows. Leather: Barley, Biscuit, Black, Buckskin, Doeskin, Isis Blue, Magnolia, Mulberry or Savile Grey. Wool tweed: Cheviot Tweed (grey), Chiltern Tweed (light brown), Cotswold Tweed (beige) or Pennine Tweed (dark brown).

Jaguar & Daimler Series III Colour Schemes, All Models (1988 model year)

Paint Colours	Leather Colours	Leather Piping
Black	Barley	–
Glacier White	Biscuit	–
Grenadier Red	Buckskin	–
Jaguar Racing Green	Charcoal	–
Westminster Blue	Doeskin	–
Talisman Silver Metallic	Doeskin	Isis Blue
Tungsten Grey Metallic	Doeskin	Mulberry
Savoy Grey Metallic (mid)	Isis Blue	–
Diamond Blue Metallic (light)	Magnolia	–
Arctic Blue Metallic (mid)	Magnolia	Isis Blue
Solent Blue Metallic (dark)	Magnolia	Mulberry
Satin Beige Metallic	Parchment	Sage Green
Bordeaux Red Metallic	Savile Grey	–
Jade Green Micatallic	Savile Grey	Mid Grey
Gunmetal Micatallic	Savile Grey	Isis Blue
Regency Red Micatallic	Savile Grey	Mulberry

Notes Jaguar offered the new option of a contrasting seat piping colour on leather-trimmed cars at extra cost, based on four trim colour schemes as listed above. Interior trim colours for leather and tweed remained unchanged. Exterior paint colours were not tied to any particular trim colours, but preferred suggestions for leather trim were as above. Wool tweed colours: Cheviot Tweed (grey), Chiltern Tweed (light brown), Cotswold Tweed (beige) or Pennine Tweed (dark brown).

Jaguar & Daimler Series III Colour Schemes, All Models (1987 model year)

Paint
Black
Nimbus White
Westminster Blue (dark)
Grenadier Red Metallic (dark)
Jaguar Racing Green Metallic
Alpine Green Metallic (light)
Arctic Blue Metallic (light)
Bordeaux Red Metallic (mid)
Crimson Metallic
Dorchester Grey Metallic (dark)
Moorland Green Metallic (dark)
Satin Beige Metallic
Silver Birch Metallic
Solent Blue Metallic (dark)
Sovereign Gold Metallic
Talisman Silver Metallic
Tungsten Metallic (mid grey)

Notes Exterior paint colours were not tied to any particular trim colours; that choice was left to the customer from the range as follows. Leather: Barley, Biscuit, Buckskin, Charcoal, Doeskin, Isis Blue, Magnolia, Mulberry or Savile Grey. Wool tweed: Cheviot Tweed (grey), Chiltern Tweed (light brown), Cotswold Tweed (beige) or Pennine Tweed (dark brown).

Earlier and later styles of Series III Vehicle Identification Number (VIN) stampings, on a metal panel by the engine cross-bracing mounting on the bulkhead.

Jaguar & Daimler Series III Colour Schemes, All Models (1989 to end of production)

Paint Colours	Leather Colours	Leather Piping	Facia Trim
Black	Barley	–	Barley
Glacier White	Charcoal	–	–
Brooklands Green (dark)	Doeskin	–	Doeskin
Westminster Blue (dark)	Doeskin	Buckskin	Doeskin
Silver Frost Metallic	Doeskin	Isis Blue	Doeskin
Tungsten Grey Metallic	Doeskin	Mulberry	Doeskin
Savoy Grey Metallic	Isis Blue	–	–
Diamond Blue Metallic (light)	Magnolia	–	Magnolia
Arctic Blue Metallic (mid)	Magnolia	Barley	Magnolia
Solent Blue Metallic (dark)	Magnolia	Isis Blue	Magnolia
Oyster Metallic	Magnolia	Mulberry	Magnolia
Bordeaux Red Metallic	Mulberry	–	–
Jade Green Micatallic	Parchment	–	Parchment
Gunmetal Micatallic	Parchment	Sage Green	Parchment
Regency Red Micatallic	Savile Grey	–	–
Tuscany Bronze Micatallic	Savile Grey	Isis Blue	–
	Savile Grey	Mid Grey	–
	Savile Grey	Mulberry	–

Notes Exterior paint colours were not tied to any particular trim colours, but preferred suggestions for leather trim were as above. Wool tweed colours were unchanged: Cheviot Tweed (grey), Chiltern Tweed (light brown), Cotswold Tweed (beige) or Pennine Tweed (dark brown). Jaguar continued to offer the option of a contrasting seat piping colour on leather-trimmed cars at extra cost, based on trim colour schemes as listed above. A new scheme from Jaguar was the bespoke treatment of facia padded top rails and surrounds. Although geared to the later XJ40 range of cars, this facia trim was also available on the Series III models from 1989 to the end of production. The standard colour was black but with the options shown above for leather-trimmed cars.

Clubs, Magazines & Books

There can be no other marque in the world better covered by clubs than Jaguar, although some of the clubs are very small and cater for niche areas of interest or are merely based on geographical area. The largest bodies of clubs are based in the UK, Europe, US and Australia.

Jaguar Daimler Heritage Trust, Jaguar Cars Ltd, Browns Lane, Allesley, Coventry CV5 9DR (tel 01203 203532). Contact, Julia Simpson. This is the official heritage body of Jaguar Cars Ltd with specific responsibilities for the upkeep of the company archives, allied material and custody of historic vehicles. A charitable trust, the organisation is based at Jaguar's Coventry headquarters with its own museum complex and administrative accommodation. The Trust can provide valuable confirmation of vehicles' history from the original factory build records, provided that current proof of ownership can be given and the appropriate small fee is paid. It also has a wealth of information on all models, including XJs. The Trust's valuable collection of XJ models includes examples of 4.2-litre Series I, Series II, Daimler Sovereign Series II, Vanden Plas Series II, ex-royal fleet Series III, 4.2-litre Series III, V12 Sovereign Series III and Daimler Double-Six Series III. The final three Series III models are the very last examples off the production line.

Clubs

The Jaguar Car Club, Barbary, Chobham Road, Horsell, Woking, Surrey GU21 4AS (tel 01483 763811). Contact, Jeff Holman. This is the smallest of the marque clubs in the UK with less than 1000 members, but with a strong interest in the racing scene. Although operating no formal registers or with clear differentiation of models, it has several XJ-based cars involved in racing.

The Jaguar Enthusiasts Club Ltd, Freepost (BS 6705), Patchway, Bristol BS12 6BR (tel 01179 698186, fax 01179 089688). Contact, Graham Searle. This is now the largest Jaguar-oriented club in the world with members in over 50 countries, with a substantial number of members owning XJ models. The Club offers discounted insurance schemes, technical advice, its own mail order business for special tools and Jaguar regalia (including books), regular national and local events, seminars, discount on RAC membership and even its own credit card. The Club's award-winning 96-page monthly magazine, *Jaguar Enthusiast*, contains a wealth of information on the cars, including many technical features and even full restorations, two XJs already having been covered in serialised form. The Club also boasts the largest classified advertisement area for Jaguars of any publication in the world.

The Jaguar Drivers Club Ltd, 18 Stuart Street, Luton, Bedfordshire LU1 2SL (tel 01582 419332). Contact, the Secretary. This is the oldest-established club for Jaguars in the UK and also has members world-wide. It has a Register for XJ models and publishes a monthly magazine, *Jaguar Driver*, with regular features on members' cars. The Club arranges an annual XJ Day for enthusiasts of the model.

The Daimler and Lanchester Owners Club, The Manor House, Trewyn, Montgomery NP7 7PG (tel 01873 890737). Contact, John Ridley. This is a long-established marque club devoted to vehicles that carry the Daimler name. Although primarily involved with the more traditional Daimler models, it now has a strong following from owners with Jaguar-Daimlers, including XJ-based models which have their own register. The Club also organises national and international events and has a monthly magazine, *The Driving Member*, which often contains articles on XJ cars.

The JCNA (Jaguar Clubs of North America), 172 Overhill Road, Stormville, NY 12582, USA (tel/fax 914 221 0293). Contact, Karen Miller. This is a central body incorporating the interests of the many clubs in the US with a strong and very enthusiastic involvement in the Jaguar scene, which includes all models of XJ. All members receive a monthly magazine, *Jaguar Journal*, produced jointly with Jaguar Cars America, and many national events and shows are organised.

Examples of owner 'packages' that came with a new car, in this case for Series II Daimler and late-model Series III Jaguar.

The Jaguar Clubs of Australia are also numerous with at least eight main organisers. Because of the vast area, they organise their own events and activities; much is co-ordinated with the Australian *Jaguar Magazine* (see below).

Magazines

Apart from the club magazines mentioned above, which are only available to club members, the following publications are available on subscription (unless otherwise stated).

Jaguar World, P. J. Publishing Ltd, PO Box 40, Hornchurch, Essex RM11 3LG (tel 01708 475593). This glossy monthly magazine with over 130 pages is specifically geared to those with an interest in Jaguar, whether new models or classics, but with a strong content for the XJ owner. There are major restorations and technical features every month, plus information on historical matters and events world-wide on the Jaguar scene. This magazine is available from newsagents or by subscription.

Jaguar Monthly, Kelsey Publishing Limited, Cudham Tithe Barn, Berrys Hill, Cudham, Kent TN16 3AG (tel 01959 541444). This is a recently-introduced 'lifestyle' magazine for owners and enthusiasts of the many Jaguar models, with particular emphasis on the XJ Series cars and later models. Major articles every month cover the running of Jaguars, latest developments from the company, model comparisons and price guides. The magazine is available from newsagents or by subscription.

Jaguar Journal, 10 Hawthorne Road, Wayne NJ 07470, USA (tel/fax 973 835 9079). This US-based bi-monthly magazine contains an average of 30 pages with articles of general interest to Jaguar owners as well as coverage of Jaguar events throughout that country.

Jaguar Magazine, PO Box 228, Holland Park, Q 4121, Australia (tel 07 3349 0322). Editor: Les Hughes. This Australian glossy Jaguar bi-monthly is produced in conjunction with Jaguar Cars Australia and the Council of Jaguar Clubs in that country. An average of over 70 pages, many in colour, cover a wide range of Jaguar interests, sometimes with specific coverage of XJ cars.

Sovereign Magazine, 45 Blondvil Street, Coventry, Warwickshire CV1 5QX. Produced quarterly, this is the official international magazine published on behalf of Jaguar Cars Ltd. This very high quality full-colour magazine has an average of 60 pages devoted to 'lifestyle' features, plus information on the latest models. Sometimes the Jaguar heritage is covered with information on the XJ ranges. Available on subscription or via Jaguar dealers.

Books

The books available on the Jaguar marque are many and varied, and continually proliferating. While most general books, to a lesser or greater extent, devote some content to the XJ Series, the following are specialist titles or those covering general topics but with a significant content for the XJ enthusiast.

Jaguar XJ – The Complete Companion by Nigel Thorley (published by Bay View Books). A softbound 160-page book that is specifically about the XJ Series I to III models and Daimler derivatives. It covers the development and history of the cars, the background to production changes, owners' views, buyers' guide, maintenance checks, specials and competitive involvement.

The XJ Series – The Complete Story by Graham Robson (published by The Crowood Press). This specifically covers all the XJ series but not in the same detail because of the need to include the XJ-S models also.

Jaguar XJ6 Purchase and Restoration by Dave Pollard (published by Haynes). A good easy-reference guide to the buying and maintenance of the six-cylinder variants in all Series.

Jaguar Enthusiasts Club XJ6 Restoration by John Williams (published by Kelsey Publishing). A publication produced after the serialisation of an XJ6 Coupé rebuild in the pages of *Jaguar Enthusiast* magazine, which covered the original purchase, bodywork, mechanical and trim aspects.

Brooklands Books. These magazine reprints come in a full range of titles covering the very first Series I XJs right through to the last of the Series IIIs. Each volume contains contemporary road tests, launch reports and long-term assessments, reprinted from magazines around the world.

Transport Source Books. A range of titles covering the V12s, the XJ6 from 1968 to 1973, and 1973 to 1979. The content is reprinted articles from contemporary magazines.

Jaguar – The Complete Works by Nigel Thorley (published by Bay View Books). A look at all Jaguar models but with specific chapters on all three Series of XJ, giving a brief history, colour photographs of each model and detailed specification and build numbers.

Jaguar – History of a Classic Marque by Philip Porter (published by Sidgwick & Jackson). Of coffee-table size, this book spans the full history of Jaguar but with good coverage on the XJ models, with contemporary pictures and information.

Jaguar Illustrated Buyers Guide by Michael Cook (published by Motorbooks International). A soft-bound work covering all the Jaguar models, this American publication has a useful section for XJ owners, with good production information and period black and white pictures.

Out-of-Print Books
At the time of writing the following titles are no longer available but are worth seeking out for their specific detail on the XJ models.

Jaguar Saloon Cars by Paul Skilleter (published by Haynes). The authoritative work on the Jaguar marque by the world's expert contains a signifi-cant amount of information on the XJ models, with historic photographs of the development of each model.

Jaguar XJ Auto History by Chris Harvey (published by Osprey). A small and handy book, one of the first published on the XJ, covering the models up to the introduction of the Series III and also including the XJ-S.

Jaguar XJ Saloons – A Collectors Guide by Paul Skilleter (published by Motor Racing Publications). Another slim volume covering history and development up to the early Series IIIs.

Jaguar Sports and Racing Cars from 1954 by Andrew Whyte (published by Haynes). A major work by the late Andrew Whyte, formal historian for Jaguar, covering the competitive history of the cars. It includes extensive information on the Broadspeed XJ Coupé racers from the '70s.

Series I/II and Series III body styles contrasted.